D0554069

112882311

Andrew Jackson

7th President of the United States

Andrew Jackson
7th President of the United States

Rebecca Stefoff

GARRETT EDUCATIONAL CORPORATION

Cover: *Official presidential portrait of Andrew Jackson by John Wesley Jarvis.* (Copyrighted by the White House Historical Association; photograph by the National Geographic Society.)

Edited and produced by Synthegraphics Corporation

Library of Congress Cataloging in Publication Data

Stefoff, Rebecca, 1951–
    Andrew Jackson, 7th president of the United States.

    (Presidents of the United States)
    Bibliography: p.
    Includes index
    Summary: A biography of the seventh President describing his frontier childhood, education, career as a soldier and politician, and his new approach to the presidency.
    1. Jackson, Andrew, 1767–1845–Juvenile literature.
2. Presidents–United States–Biography–Juvenile literature. [1. Jackson, Andrew, 1787–1845.
2. Presidents] I. Title. II. Series.
E382.S73 1988 973.5'6'0924 [B] [92] 87-32878
ISBN 0-944483-08-9

Contents

Chronology for Andrew Jackson

1767 Born on March 15 in the Waxhaw region of the Carolinas

1780–1781 Served in informal local militia in Revolutionary War; was wounded by a British officer

1787 Certified to practice law in North Carolina

1788 Moved to Nashville, Tennessee

1791 Married Rachel Donelson Robards in August (second ceremony performed in 1794)

1796 Elected as Tennessee's first delegate to the U.S. House of Representatives

1797 Elected to the U.S. Senate

1798–1804 Served as a superior court judge in Tennessee

1812 Commanded company of Tennessee volunteers in War of 1812

1815 Defeated British at New Orleans at end of War of 1812

1817–1818 Attacked Seminole Indians and Spanish in Florida

1821 Appointed first governor of Florida Territory

1823–1825 Served as U.S. senator from Tennessee; lost his first presidential campaign to John Quincy Adams

1829–1837 Served as seventh President of the United States

1845 Died on June 8 at his home, The Hermitage, near Nashville, Tennessee

Indian fighter and hero of the Battle of New Orleans, Andrew Jackson was one of the most popular Presidents the United States has ever had. One rival claimed that Jackson could have been President "for life" if he had wanted. (Library of Congress.)

Chapter 1

The Hero of New Orleans

The winter of 1814–1815 was a season of fear and confusion in the American South. The United States and England had been at war since 1812, and the United States was under attack. Despite some notable victories, the Americans had been hard pressed to hold their own. British forces had even marched into Washington, D.C., in the summer of 1814, setting fire to the grand new buildings of the young nation's capital. So desperate was the situation that some people called the War of 1812 "America's second war of independence."

Fighting had raged in the north, along the Canadian border, and there had been naval battles off the eastern seacoast. Now, in late 1814, the United States and England had begun peace talks in the Belgian city of Ghent, but military action still continued in the New World, as the North American continent was known to Europeans.

The fighting had now shifted to the South. Rumors had been flying for weeks that the British were going to try to capture New Orleans. The city, which had been purchased from France in 1803 as part of the Louisiana Purchase, was a great prize. Whoever controlled it also controlled the Mississippi River Valley—and America's avenue to the West.

A HERO TAKES CHARGE

By November 1814, the people of New Orleans were in a fever of dismay and uncertainty. They had few weapons and soldiers, and no leader or plan of defense. Terrifying news arrived: Lieutenant General Sir Edward Pakenham and 7,500 British troops had set sail from the British island of Jamaica, in the Caribbean, and were bound for New Orleans. Panic swept the city. Then, on December 1, an unlikely looking hero rode into the city at the head of a ragtag army of frontiersmen.

He was tall and extremely gaunt, with a thin, careworn face and a mane of gray hair. He wore a shabby uniform and unpolished boots. Although ill with dysentery, he sat stiffly erect in his saddle. His men, who idolized him, told in guarded whispers of his fearsome temper and his heroic feats against the Indians. His name was Andrew Jackson, and he held the rank of major general in the U.S. Army. To his men, however, he was known as "Old Hickory," because they knew he was as tough and unyielding as seasoned hickory wood.

Jackson arrived in New Orleans to find the city practically defenseless. He quickly declared martial law, which gave him, as military commander, the power to issue orders to the civilian population during the emergency. Although this action was later criticized, it enabled Jackson to assemble the city's defenses quickly.

"Dirty Shirts" Against "Redcoats"

The British were expected to send a massive force against New Orleans, so Jackson promptly sent out a call for reinforcements. Unfortunately, many of the volunteers who answered his call did not have uniforms or weapons. Nearly 2,400 Kentuckians came, but only 700 of them had rifles—a fact that amazed Jackson, who declared, "I have never seen a Kentuckian without a gun and a pack of cards and a bottle of whiskey in my life."

By the time Jackson's force was marshalled, it numbered about 4,500 men. They were a colorful crew: a few regular soldiers in threadbare uniforms; volunteers and militiamen from throughout the South; frontiersmen from Tennessee and Kentucky, with long rifles, buckskin jackets, and coonskin caps; and French, Spanish, and Portuguese settlers who had made their homes in the Louisiana Territory.

Jackson's army included the first black Americans to serve in the U.S. militia – about 200 freedmen, or former slaves. Some people had argued against giving the freedmen weapons, fearing that it would encourage a slave revolt. But Jackson stood firm and ordered that the blacks be given the same treatment and pay as all other volunteers.

The most colorful and controversial part of the army was a group of pirates led by Jean Lafitte. For years, the pirates had hidden in a region of the Louisiana coast known as Barataria, from which they occasionally emerged on errands of piracy and smuggling. Lafitte had refused an offer of $30,000 and a captaincy in the British navy to help the British capture New Orleans. Instead, he offered his services to Jackson in return for pardons for himself and his men. Jackson accepted the offer, which President James Madison later confirmed. Although some of the city's stuffier citizens grumbled that the Baratarians belonged in jail and not in the army, Jackson's faith in Lafitte was sound. The pirate leader and his men were to prove valuable allies.

The British troops under Pakenham were well-armed and highly trained. The Americans called them "Redcoats" because of their trim, bright-red uniforms. The Redcoats, on the other hand, referred to the poorly equipped, hodgepodge American force as "Dirty Shirts." Under the leadership of Old Hickory, however, the Dirty Shirts prepared to do their best against the Redcoats.

A Wall of Mud

Jackson wasn't sure where and when Pakenham would attack New Orleans, which stretched for some distance along the east bank of the Mississippi River. On December 23, he received news that 1,800 British troops had advanced to an undefended bayou, or creek, that led into a marsh about seven miles from the city. Jackson knew that the enemy could approach the city only along a narrow strip of land between the river and the marsh. He also knew that he could not hold the city by force of arms, so he moved swiftly to set up the only possible defense.

First, Jackson led his troops in a night attack on the enemy force, halting its advance. Then, while the British brought up reinforcements, increasing their army to about 10,000 battle-trained soldiers, Jackson led his men to a point about five miles from New Orleans. There he ordered them to build a rampart, or wall, out of mud and logs to block the narrow strip of land that led to the city.

Thousands of slaves worked feverishly side by side with the soldiers, cutting wood, dragging logs, and hauling buckets of earth. The city's businessmen and landowners helped, too. Within 24 hours, the wall was finished. It stretched for about 1,000 yards from the river to the swamp. Behind it crouched Jackson's army, with about a dozen cannon. Behind them the city of New Orleans waited in suspense to learn its fate.

THE BATTLE OF NEW ORLEANS

The first British attack on Jackson's defensive rampart came on December 28. American cannon fire drove the British back, but the Redcoats brought cannon from their warships moored in the Gulf of Mexico. On New Year's Day, 1815, the

British launched a furious bombardment, but the American defenses held.

Unable to breach the American lines, Pakenham waited until all of his reinforcements had arrived. For a week, the American troops and the city also waited with growing tension for the eventual attack. Finally, as dawn broke on the cold, foggy morning of January 8 and Jackson was pacing along the top of his mud-walled rampart, he gazed toward the British camp less than two miles away. At 6:00 A.M. he saw a rocket flare against the still-dark sky and remarked calmly to his aides, "That, I believe, is their signal to advance."

Jackson was correct. Soon the waiting Americans heard the shrill sound of bagpipes and the beating of British drums. The fog lifted to reveal two immense columns of Redcoats advancing toward the wall.

At Jackson's command, the Americans fired their cannon. The cannonballs cut bloody paths through the British ranks, but the Redcoat advance continued relentlessly. Again and again the cannon were loaded and fired, mowing down hundreds of British soldiers. The disciplined Redcoats, however, continued to attack; those in back climbed over their fallen comrades to approach the wall. But as soon as they neared the rampart, they were within range of musket fire, and the sharpshooters of Kentucky and Tennessee picked them off one at a time.

British Blunders

Several things went wrong with the British attack. One British unit was supposed to have crossed the river before dawn to capture an American artillery position. But it was swept downstream by the strong current and missed the battle entirely. Another group was supposed to have led the advance, carrying ladders for climbing the wall. This group also was

This drawing of the Battle of New Orleans shows the death of Sir Edward Pakenham, the British general. Behind him, the British forces are clustered below Jackson's rampart, from which the Americans can fire down upon them. The Stars and Stripes wave at both ends of the rampart. (Library of Congress.)

not in position when the signal for the British to attack was given.

No one knows how the British might have fared if they had not bungled their attack so badly. It is likely, though, that the American defenses would have held. The American position was clearly strong enough to carry the day, even with a smaller force.

The battle lasted barely half an hour. Under heavy barrage from the cannon mounted on the wall, the Redcoats slowed their advance. Pakenham then rushed to the head of one of the two columns to rally his discouraged men. He was shot twice and killed. The tide had turned against the British, who soon withdrew.

The British losses were terrible: 1,262 men wounded, 484 captured, and nearly 300 killed. In addition to Pakenham, two generals were also killed, and many other officers died on the field as well.

In contrast, the Americans suffered remarkably few losses, although accounts differ slightly. Jackson claimed seven men killed and six wounded, but other reports say that 14 men were killed, 39 wounded, and 18 captured. Even the higher numbers are quite low considering the number of British losses and the importance of the battle.

The Treaty of Ghent

The Battle of New Orleans was the greatest land victory of the War of 1812. Surprisingly, though, it had no effect on the outcome of the war. In fact, the war had actually ended before the battle was even fought.

After three years of fighting, the United States and England finally reached agreement on peace terms just before Christmas of 1814. The Treaty of Ghent was signed in the Belgian city by representatives of the United States and En-

Americans were horrified and frightened when British forces invaded Washington in August of 1814, during the War of 1812. The British set fire to the Capitol and other buildings while President James Madison and other statesmen fled the city. (Library of Congress.)

gland on December 24. The war was over—but, because there were no telegraphs or telephones to carry the news, no one in the United States would know about the peace treaty for weeks. In the meantime, Andrew Jackson became a hero and the darling of the nation.

The Making of a Legend

Jackson's overwhelming victory at New Orleans restored American confidence, which had suffered serious blows during the war, especially when the British invaded Washington, D.C. Because news of the peace treaty reached most Americans at about the same time as news of the Battle of New Orleans, many people believed that the battle had actually ended the war in triumph for the United States. Grateful for something to be proud of, the American people gave Jackson the credit he deserved for winning the battle.

Jackson's judgment and leadership had proved sound. The pirates he trusted had manned the cannon during the British attack; it is possible that they carried the day for the Americans. And his mud wall had held off the best that the British could send against it.

Admiring tales about Old Hickory and the events of the battle soon were being told at firesides and in taverns across the land. One popular song, called "The Hunters of Kentucky," paid tribute to Jackson's frontiersmen fighters and his mud wall:

> Behind it stood our little force—
> None wished it to be greater;
> For every man was half a horse,
> And half an alligator.

This and other songs and poems glorified Jackson and his bold defense. He received official recognition, too, in the form of a vote of thanks and a gold medal from the U.S. Congress. But less than a month after being voted the gold medal he received attention of a less welcome kind. Judge Dominick A. Hall of the New Orleans district court fined Jackson $1,000 for contempt of court.

The penalty was imposed for Jackson's declaration of martial law in New Orleans before the battle. Although Jackson had believed the action necessary for the defense of the city, he had been in violation of a court order and now had to pay the fine. That did not reduce his feelings of pride and triumph, however, and it certainly did not lessen public admiration of him.

In the wake of the Battle of New Orleans, Old Hickory became a symbol of distinctive American strengths and virtues: stubbornness, individuality, imagination, and fierce patriotic pride. Suddenly, he was perhaps the best-known and best-loved figure in the United States. His fame would one day carry him to the highest office in the land—but he had many battles still to fight before he reached the presidency.

Chapter 2

A Frontier Youth

In 1765, a ship going to America carried a married couple and their two infant sons from Carrickfergus, in northern Ireland. The couple were Andrew Jackson's parents, Andrew and Elizabeth Hutchinson Jackson; the boys were Hugh, three years old, and Robert, a baby. Like many immigrants to the New World, Andrew and Elizabeth Jackson brought few possessions – and the dream of making a more prosperous life for themselves and their family in their new land.

Elizabeth's sister, Mrs. James Crawford, had invited the Jacksons to settle near her and her husband in the Waxhaw region, on the border between North Carolina and South Carolina. Life was difficult here on the frontier, but Andrew Jackson, who had always worked as a laborer for someone else, was glad for the chance to work for himself. He began by building a log cabin for his family along the Crawfords' branch of Waxhaw Creek.

The nearest road was the boundary between North and South Carolina, and in later years both states would claim Andrew Jackson as a native son. Jackson always said that he was born in South Carolina and, although the exact site of his birth is unknown, the evidence favors South Carolina's claim.

This old illustration shows Jackson's birthplace in the Waxhaw region as it probably appeared around the time of the American Revolution. In later years, both North and South Carolina claimed him as a native son, but South Carolina's claim is generally accepted. (Library of Congress.)

A RUGGED CHILDHOOD

Two years later, in 1767, Andrew Jackson was killed in an accident while clearing the land. Elizabeth Jackson was now a widow, one of the most difficult situations a woman could face in Colonial times. She could not work the land without help, she had two young children to feed—and she was pregnant with a third. Fortunately, the Crawfords gave Elizabeth and her children a home. Elizabeth helped with the household chores and, when the boys grew older, they helped with the farm work.

On March 15, 1767, a month after his father's death, Andrew Jackson was born. Young Andrew grew up tall, slender, blue-eyed, and sandy-haired. He had a quick temper and frequently fought with much larger boys—and he often beat them. His mother hoped he would become a Presbyterian minister, but Andrew showed little interest in such a career. He was more interested in sports and rough-housing.

The frontier offered little in the way of schooling, but Andrew attended classes in the Waxhaw Presbyterian Church. He learned to read and write—rare skills for children and adults alike in those days. However, he never mastered the fine points of grammar and remained a terrible speller to the end of his days. Nevertheless, he was a persuasive and eloquent speaker, who made up in fire and emotion what he lacked in grammatical elegance.

Independence and Revolution

Like most farm communities of the day, the Waxhaw region had "public readers," who read aloud to the people the news in Philadelphia newspapers. Andrew later recalled that he was chosen "as often as any grown man" to be the reader.

One such occasion had a powerful effect on Andrew. In 1776, at the age of nine, he read the newly adopted Declaration of Independence to his mother and their neighbors. He had inherited a hatred of the British from his Irish parents and was excited by the idea of fighting for freedom from England. His oldest brother, Hugh, went off to fight in the Revolutionary War. But Andrew was too young to take part in these stirring events.

Two years later, Andrew was sent to a boarding school in a nearby settlement. There, he and other boys studied reading, writing, grammar, and geography. He remained a poor student, however, and was more interested in news of the war than in his schoolbooks. Some of the war news was tragic. In 1779, the Jacksons learned that Hugh had been killed in a battle. In the meantime, the war moved closer to their home.

In 1780, British troops invaded South Carolina, setting off a fierce civil war in which Tories, who remained loyal to England, battled against the patriots, who wanted independence. Neighbors and even family members were sometimes turned against one another by their conflicting loyalties.

One tragedy of the war was the Waxhaw Massacre, in which 113 patriots were killed during a surprise British raid. As a result of the massacre, Andrew's hatred of the British grew even greater. He was now 13 years old — old enough to join the militia, a volunteer force of patriots. He was made a courier, one of the messengers who raced between militia headquarters and battlegrounds carrying dispatches for officers. Andrew took his responsibilities as a courier very seriously and carried out his duties faithfully. He also took careful note of military decisions and their effectiveness, storing insights that would be helpful to him years later when he had his own command.

Andrew's other brother, Robert, had also joined the militia. The two boys were present at the Battle of Hanging Rock, in which their uncle, James Crawford, was wounded. They escaped unharmed, but their luck soon turned.

British Boots

In April of 1781, Andrew and Robert were involved in a skirmish with a British raiding party. They fled, hoping to escape capture, and hid in a nearby house. But a Tory neighbor had seen them and alerted the British to their hiding place. The boys were captured.

While the raiding party searched the house for more fugitives, one of the British officers ordered Andrew to clean his muddy boots. Andrew drew himself up proudly and replied, "Sir, I am a prisoner of war, and claim to be treated as such." The angry officer lashed out with his sword, and Andrew threw up his hand to protect himself. The blade slashed his hand to the bone and cut him on the head, creating deep wounds that would leave lifelong scars. The British then ordered the two boys to march to a prison camp at Camden, South Carolina, about 40 miles away.

Revolutionary War prison camps were deadly places. The captors on both sides gave little or no medical aid to their prisoners, who were tended only by civilian volunteers and fellow soldiers. In addition, diseases spread like wildfire through the camps. The Jackson brothers soon contracted smallpox, which was often fatal at that time. They were seriously ill when their mother learned of their imprisonment and arranged for their release through an exchange of prisoners.

A BOY ALONE

On the way home from Camden, Robert died of smallpox and exposure. Andrew was near death for weeks, but he pulled through. When his recovery seemed certain, his mother left for Charleston, South Carolina, where she was needed to help care for sick relatives aboard British prison ships. Andrew never saw her again—she died in Charleston of cholera, a disease she caught while nursing sick prisoners.

At 14 years of age, Andrew had lost his father, his two brothers, and his mother. He later said that he felt "utterly alone." The Revolutionary War was now over. Independence had been won. For young Andrew Jackson, however, the end of the war also meant starting a new life without his family.

Choosing a Future

Andrew spent the next three years with various relatives, first in Charleston, then in the Waxhaw region. For a time he attended an academy in Charlotte, North Carolina, where he applied a little polish to his frontier education. As always, however, he spent less time studying than he spent carousing. He also added gambling and brawling to his pastimes.

Although his immediate family was dead, Andrew had plenty of relatives to offer him hospitality. He also had relatives in the Old World (Europe), as he was reminded when he received an inheritance of 300 British pounds on the death of a grandfather in Ireland. In Colonial times, this was a considerable fortune, more than enough to give young Andrew an education, a home, and a livelihood. But the money was soon spent on fine clothes and gambling, leaving Andrew nearly penniless. However, he was able to earn a living by teaching school in the Waxhaw area in 1783. For as rudimentary as his own education had been, he still possessed greater learning than most of his countrymen.

By this time, Andrew had begun to consider his future. He did not want to be a farmer; he knew that his father and other relatives had been killed or prematurely aged by the hard life of farming. Moreover, he was too ambitious to settle for a life as a schoolmaster; it would give him only a bare living and keep him too poor to enjoy the sporting life he fancied. So, at the age of 17, he decided upon a career in law.

Attorney Jackson

In 1784, Andrew moved to Salisbury, North Carolina, and took up the study of law with Spruce McCay, a wealthy and well-known lawyer. At that time, aspiring lawyers did not go to law school. Instead, they learned about law by studying and working in a law office such as McCay's. Andrew learned much during the two years he spent with McCay. He found a lifelong friend in John McNairy, also a student in the same law office. McNairy's tastes were similar to Andrew's, and the two young men spent their free time at horse races, cockfights, and taverns.

After two years with McCay, Andrew spent a year studying in the law firm of Colonel John Stokes, who was famous for the large silver knob he wore in place of a hand that had been lost in the war. Stokes would pound the knob like a gavel on a judge's desk during courtroom arguments. Despite his showmanship, however, he was a competent lawyer and taught Andrew much.

In 1787, Andrew Jackson was ready to put his studies to the test. He passed the bar examination, which meant that he was certified to practice law in North Carolina. But because the state already had an abundance of attorneys, Andrew and John McNairy decided to take their new skills to the frontier, where lawyers were always in demand to settle land claims and other disputes. They set off westward on the Cumberland Trail and headed across the Appalachian Mountains for the western district of North Carolina—the region that later would become the state of Tennessee.

Chapter 3

Lawyer and Politician

When Jackson and McNairy set out for Tennessee in 1788, the region was still on the edge of the untamed western frontier. Their 300-mile journey was full of adventures. At one point, they were forced to ride like the wind to escape from a hunting party of Cherokee Indians. Later, Jackson had to shoot a wildcat that attacked one of his horses.

When the two young men reached Jonesboro, a town in what was to become eastern Tennessee, they quickly found work. Jackson was appointed public prosecutor. He and McNairy didn't remain in Jonesboro long, however. Soon after their arrival, the first wagon road to the new town of Nashville was opened, and the two attorneys were part of the first party to travel on the new highway. McNairy had been appointed a judge in the new district's superior court. Jackson was content to follow his friend, knowing that where there is a judge, lawyers are always needed. They arrived in Nashville in October of 1788.

FRONTIER LIFE AND BUSINESS

Nashville was a raw frontier settlement, exposed to the danger of attack by the Cherokee, Shawnee, and Choctaw Indians of the region. Although many Tennesseans had fought bravely in the Revolutionary War, the area had not yet achieved statehood. Some parts of it were claimed by North Carolina, some parts were federal territory, and one portion of the future state had even attempted briefly to set itself up as the state of Franklin. This uncertainty meant plenty of work for an ambitious lawyer, because many people took the law rather lightly.

Jackson was kept busy with lawsuits against people who had failed to pay their bills. In addition, he received many commissions to draw up or transfer land deeds, as everyone was speculating furiously in land investments. Before long, Jackson found himself the master of a thriving legal practice. He also became the friend and ally of a powerful group of landowners and merchants. For the next 30 years, he would be backed by this group in the politics of Tennessee.

Nashville itself consisted of a wooden stockade for the soldiers of the local army unit; the citizens were expected to gather inside the stockade if the town was attacked. The community also boasted a number of log cabins and rough buildings, including the tiny courthouse where Jackson's cases were heard. Deciding not to live right in town, Jackson found living quarters in a boardinghouse about 10 miles away. There he made another lifelong friend: John Overton, a young lawyer from Virginia. There also, soon after moving in, he was involved in a serious romance.

Courtship and Two Marriages

The boardinghouse where Jackson lived was owned by Mrs. Rachel Stockley Donelson, a widow. Her daughter, a pretty dark-haired girl also named Rachel, was married to Captain Lewis Robards, an army officer from Kentucky. The marriage was an unhappy one. Although Rachel had been married for five years when Jackson met her, she had recently left her husband after a violent quarrel and returned to her mother's house.

Before long, Jackson was attracted by Rachel's quiet beauty; she, in turn, admired his courtesy as well as his entertaining dinner-table conversation. They were no more than friends, however, when Rachel's husband came to live in the house, hoping to save the marriage. But another quarrel soon followed, and Robards left. Later, Robards sent word to his wife that he had received permission from the Virginia legislature to sue her for divorce. Rachel misunderstood the message, however, and believed that she had already been divorced.

In the meantime, Rachel had moved south to Natchez, a city along the Mississippi River in the Mississippi Territory. When Jackson heard of her divorce, he followed her to Natchez, determined to marry her. They were married in Natchez in August of 1791, after which they returned to Nashville and set up a new home. Two years later, the couple discovered that Rachel had not, in fact, been legally divorced at the time of her marriage to Jackson. This meant that Jackson and Rachel had not been married legally. To repair the situation as quickly as possible, they were married again, in January of 1794, after Rachel's divorce had been declared final.

The marriage was to last for 37 happy years. But the confused circumstances of their courtship and marriage

Jackson married Rachel Donelson Robards twice, in 1791 and 1794. They were happily married for 37 years. She died after his election to the presidency but before he took office. (Library of Congress.)

haunted them for a long time, giving rise to many rumors and much gossip. Jackson's personal and political enemies would make unkind references to Rachel's bigamy or to Jackson's illegal marriage; some of the worst gossips even said that Robards had divorced Rachel after learning that she and Jackson had been having an illicit love affair. The young lawyer and future President reacted to these remarks and accusations with anger, and often found himself having to defend his wife's honor.

Law, Business, and Politics

Jackson's marriage may have raised some eyebrows, but the Donelsons were a prominent and well-to-do family. They had a higher social position than did Jackson's own family. Partly through their influence and partly through his own talents, Jackson grew to be one of the most important lawyers in the area. Before long, he was handling as many as half of all the local court cases. His friend McNairy also helped Jackson's career by appointing him prosecuting attorney for the district.

Money in the territory was scarce, though, so Jackson sometimes accepted deeds to land as a substitute for cash in payment for his legal fees. In this way, he became one of the district's important landowners. In 1796, he bought a 650-acre plantation called Hunter's Hill, about 12 miles outside of Nashville. There, years later, he would build a stately mansion.

Because he was by nature adventurous, Jackson enjoyed the lively boom-and-bust economy of the frontier. He began to invest in land and horses, and he hired workers to raise cotton on some of his land. At that time, land speculation was the source of many great fortunes. Jackson, for example, was able to buy land for as little as 10 cents an acre, later selling it for as much as three dollars an acre.

But Jackson's fortunes followed a boom-and-bust cycle — some years would be extremely prosperous, only to be fol-

Jackson built this mansion, The Hermitage, a few miles outside of Nashville. It was an elegant home with a large plantation that was worked by slaves. Today it is maintained as a museum of Jackson's life and achievements. (Library of Congress.)

lowed by much leaner ones. Between one year and the next, Jackson might change from being one of the richest men in Nashville to feeling the pinch of his debts.

While Jackson's business and property were developing, events were occurring that propelled him toward politics. In 1790, when North Carolina gave up its claim to its western district, President George Washington appointed North Carolinian Willie Blount to serve as governor of the territory. Statehood was now in the air. People began to think about future appointments and elections.

Because Jackson was well-liked by many influential landowners and businessmen in the region, they started urging him to consider politics. Then, in 1791, he received two new appointments: one was as attorney general of the nearby Mero District; the other was as judge-advocate of the Davidson County militia. Although the latter position did not bring much profit, it did get Jackson involved with the military once again.

By 1795 it had become certain that the territory was about to become a new state in the Union. A convention was called to draw up a state constitution. Because Tennessee's constitution was to be modeled after that of North Carolina, which Jackson had studied during his legal training, he was asked to be a delegate to the convention. His contributions to the convention are unknown, but some historians say that it was Andrew Jackson who proposed the name "Tennessee" for the new state.

SERVING THE NEW STATE

Tennessee was granted statehood in 1796. When the state's first elections were held that same year, Jackson was chosen as Tennessee's first delegate to the U.S. House of Representatives, which met in Philadelphia at that time.

Jackson's first congressional stint was unremarkable. During his three months in the House, he made just two speeches. He achieved notice only when he voted against a motion to give George Washington a tribute at the conclusion of his presidency. Jackson criticized some of President Washington's policies, especially the Jay Treaty of 1794, which established peace with England. Jackson's hatred of the British was still as fierce as ever, and he felt that the treaty was too favorable to England.

Later in his life, this vote against the tribute caused Jackson some embarrassment, when it was said that no man who had voted against the "father of his country" should become President. At the time, though, it didn't appear to bother the voters of Tennessee.

When his first short term in Congress ended in early 1797, Jackson refused to seek re-election. Instead, he returned to Tennessee vowing that he wanted no more of politics. Later that same year, however, he was elected to the U.S. Senate. But after only a year in Philadelphia, he went back to Tennessee on a leave of absence from his senatorial duties and, while at home, resigned from office.

Jackson resigned from the Senate for several reasons. For one, he found the pace of life in Philadelphia to be too slow and sedate for his tastes; he preferred the more hectic life of the frontier. It is also possible that he felt out of place as a rough westerner among the cultivated and sophisticated easterners in Congress. In addition, he felt financial pressures and wanted to raise some money by returning to his law practice.

Finally, Jackson missed Rachel and their family. Although they never had children of their own, they adopted the four-day-old son of Rachel's brother and renamed him Andrew Jackson, Jr.; they also raised two other sons of the same brother after his death. Later, the Jacksons would raise a great-nephew of Rachel's named Andrew Jackson Hutchings and an orphaned Creek Indian boy whom they named Lyncoyer Jackson.

Judge Jackson

Upon returning to Nashville, Jackson was offered an appointment as one of the judges of the state superior court, with a salary of $600 a year—quite a bit of money in the late 18th century. This position eased his financial difficulties and enabled him to stay closer to home. He served for six years, riding a circuit between district courts in Nashville, Knoxville, Jonesboro, and other communities. Upon reaching a courthouse, Jackson would take his long, black judge's robes from his saddlebag and administer justice.

Although not a learned judge, Jackson was an energetic one. An observer later described his legal opinions as "unlearned, sometimes ungrammatical," and "generally right." He was also fearless. On one occasion, a gunman named Russell Bean held a crowd hostage outside a courthouse. Judge Jackson emerged, drew his own weapon, and sternly ordered Bean to drop his gun. To everyone's amazement, Bean did so. The gunman later said, "I looked him in the eye, and I saw 'shoot.' "

No doubt Bean was quite right. During the past few years, Jackson had developed a reputation as a duelist. Dueling was illegal in some states, and many people opposed it as immoral or dangerous. Nevertheless, it was not uncommon for men to meet on the dueling-ground to settle a dispute or avenge an insult. In many cases, the duel was fought simply to satisfy a sense of honor, with no intention to kill. In such instances, the duelists inflicted minor wounds on one another or fired into the air.

Jackson's hot temper made him quick to sense an insult

Although dueling was illegal in many states, men still resorted to it to settle arguments. Jackson became a famous duelist, especially after killing Charles Dickinson on a dueling-ground in Kentucky. (Library of Congress.)

and equally quick to issue a challenge. He had fought his first duel in Tennessee soon after arriving there in 1788; neither he nor his opponent, Waightstill Avery, a North Carolina lawyer, was injured. It is not known how many duels followed. Often his friends were able to talk him out of a challenge; in other cases, his opponents apologized or settled their differences—especially after Jackson's reputation as a duelist began to grow. Some historians estimate, however, that Jackson may have fought as many as 100 duels. In all of these contests, only one was fatal.

The Dickinson Duel

Jackson's most famous duel took place in 1806. It pitted him against Charles Dickinson, a notorious speculator and slave trader. The dispute between the two men started with a disagreement over a bet. Matters grew more serious when Dickinson called Jackson "a worthless scoundrel . . . and a coward." To top it off, Dickinson made some insulting remarks about Rachel. That was all Jackson needed to hear. Even though Dickinson was known as an excellent pistol shot, Jackson issued a challenge, and it was promptly accepted.

The duelists met on May 30, across the state line in Kentucky. They stood the regulation 24 feet apart, pistols pointed downward. With his opponent staring him in the face, Jackson coolly calculated the odds. He realized that Dickinson, the superior shot, would probably shoot first and hit him—but he gambled that the wound would not be fatal. If he survived Dickinson's shot, dueling etiquette would allow him to take a slow, careful return shot.

It happened just as Jackson expected. Dickinson got off the first shot and struck Jackson in the chest. At this point, Jackson demonstrated the qualities of coolness and determination which were to make him famous in battle. He did not

This woodcut originally appeared in a book about Jackson that was published in 1834. It shows a glorified and exaggerated version of Jackson's encounter with the Benton brothers in 1812. The artist has given Jackson and a friend military uniforms. (Library of Congress.)

Jackson and the Benton Brothers

In 1812, Jackson was involved in a duel that became famous. It all started when Jackson served as a second to his friend, William Carroll, who had been challenged to a duel by a man named Jesse Benton. When the duel took place, Benton fired first and missed. He turned to run away, but Carroll shot him in the seat of his pants—a wound that was not dangerous, but was very embarrassing,

Benton's brother, Thomas Hart Benton, was outraged at his brother's humiliation. He heard that Jackson had been involved and issued a rude challenge to him. Jackson refused and threatened to horsewhip Thomas Hart Benton if their paths ever crossed.

Their paths crossed a few days later at the Nashville post office, where Jackson spotted both of the Benton brothers. When he shouted at them, Thomas Hart Benton reached into his pocket, and Jackson drew his gun. Thomas Hart Benton then backed off, but Jesse Benton shot Jackson in the left shoulder and arm. Doctors who were called to the scene said they might have to amputate the arm, but Jackson's last words before fainting were an order: "I shall keep my arm." He kept the arm, although one bullet remained lodged in it and caused him considerable pain until surgeons were able to remove it 20 years later.

The Bentons knew that Jackson would be after them as soon as he recovered from his wound, so they fled from Nashville. Thomas

Hart Benton wound up in Missouri, was elected to the U.S. Senate, and held that office for 30 years. Later in the political careers of both men, Benton became one of Jackson's staunchest supporters.

fall. Instead, he merely clapped one hand to his chest to control the flow of blood, raised his own gun, and took aim. The horrified Dickinson could either stand and await the shot or run and be branded a coward. He stood his ground, and Jackson shot him below the ribs. Dickinson bled to death in a few minutes.

Jackson, too, bled freely. Several of his ribs were broken, and the bullet had lodged too close to his heart to be removed. He recovered, though, and carried Dickinson's bullet in his chest for the rest of his life. When someone congratulated him on his good luck in being able to kill Dickinson despite a chest wound, Jackson replied calmly that he would have killed him even if he had been shot in the brain.

A Frontier Gentleman

Such dramatic events were rare, not daily, occurrences. Jackson's life at this point was one of hard work and constant business activity. Because he had many debts and his creditors were demanding payment, he resigned his judgeship in 1804 to devote all his energies to business ventures and to his plantation. He sold much of Hunter's Hill, keeping only the portion where he built his own house, which he called The Hermitage.

In 1805, Jackson and John Hutchings, a relative of

Rachel, established a general store at Clover Bottom, near The Hermitage. Jackson built a stable near the store and bought several racehorses. Soon he was adding to his income with fairly steady winnings on his horses. His political career seemed to be over. Politics entered his life only in the form of lively discussions with his friends over the misguided acts of Presidents James Madison and James Monroe.

Jackson had tried and failed to obtain the coveted appointment as governor of the Louisiana Territory. Now he appeared to be settling into the comfortable life of a frontier gentlemen, lawyer, storekeeper, and sportsman. But all that was soon to change, as Andrew Jackson was about to become the most famous military leader of his generation.

Chapter 4

Old Hickory

Jackson's only military experience prior to 1802 had been his brief spell as a teenaged militia courier during the Revolutionary War. But he had always taken a keen interest in military matters and was proud of his minor connection as judge-advocate with the Davidson Country militia. Then, in 1802, he achieved a much more important position: major general of the Tennessee militia, the most desirable post in the state after the governorship.

Although the office was an elected one, Jackson owed his success in getting it partly to his friendship with Archibald Roane, a powerful Tennessee politician. Roane had just become governor, following John Sevier, who had held the governorship for three terms. Because the state constitution forbade him from serving a fourth term as governor, Sevier ran for major general of the militia. Like Jackson, Sevier was very popular with Tennesseans. When the election ended in a tie, it fell to the new governor to cast the deciding vote. Roane voted for his longtime friend, Jackson.

Jackson had no military experience and no particular qualifications for the post. At the time, however, no one expected his military duties to be very demanding. The United States was at peace with other nations, and the Indian wars had quieted down. During his first 10 years as major general, Jackson's activities with the militia were largely administrative or ceremonial.

TREASON IN TEXAS

Jackson did become embroiled in political matters during the early 1800s, however. It all started when he received a distinguished visitor at The Hermitage in 1806. The visitor was Aaron Burr, who had been the Vice-President of the United States from 1801 to 1805, during President Thomas Jefferson's first term.

Burr was notorious for having killed Alexander Hamilton, the former secretary of the treasury, in a duel in 1804. Both his political career and his social respectability were finished. But Jackson was probably too impressed by Burr's fame and sophistication to be aware of just how dubious his visitor's current status really was. He had met and admired Burr when they were both serving in Congress in the 1790s. Now he was flattered by the other man's show of friendship. Burr had a great and daring plan, he said, and he wanted Jackson's help.

Looking Westward

These were the years of great expansion to the West. The Louisiana Territory had been purchased from France in 1803, immediately doubling the size of the United States and opening up huge new tracts of unknown land to explorers and settlers. And beyond the Louisiana Territory stretched mile after mile of mysterious wilderness all the way from the Rocky Mountains to the Pacific coast.

Americans were intensely curious about these remote regions of the continent. The Lewis and Clark Expedition had set off in 1805 to explore the Louisiana Territory and pioneer a route to the Pacific. Many people began to feel that it was America's destiny to colonize the West. Burr's plan took advantage of these feelings of nationalism.

Meriwether Lewis and William Clark, here shown talking to western Indians in a drawing from 1810, led the first expedition to explore the western regions of the Louisiana Territory and beyond to the Pacific Ocean. At about the same time, former Vice-President Aaron Burr tried to embroil Jackson in a plot to invade the West. (Library of Congress.)

Burr was gathering support for an expedition down the Mississippi River. His plan concerned the area to the southwest of the Louisiana Territory known as Texas. At that time, Texas was Spanish territory. Jackson, like many Americans, resented this Spanish presence on the very doorstep of the United States. He believed that Americans should be free to expand all the way across the continent, and the Spanish presented a barrier to such expansion. But in spite of his strong desire for westward expansion, Jackson knew that violating the treaty that the United States had with Spain would be both against international law and an act of treason against his own government.

Burr appeared to suggest otherwise, however. He claimed to have secret permission from President Jefferson for a march into the southwest to drive the Spanish away from the frontier. As head of the Tennessee militia, Jackson could be very helpful in this plan.

At first, Jackson was excited by the idea. He knew that the West was threatened by Spanish forces across the border. He also welcomed the notion of conquering Texas and adding it to the United States. He gave some of the help Burr asked for, purchasing supplies for the expedition and ordering his men to build two boats for carrying troops down the Mississippi River.

Before long, however, Jackson began to have second thoughts. He learned that Burr's associate in the venture was Major General James Wilkinson, governor of the Louisiana Territory, who had a reputation for shady dealing. Later, in fact, it was learned that Wilkinson had been a paid agent of Spain while holding office in the United States. So poorly was Wilkinson regarded that Jackson became suspicious of Burr's good intentions and withdrew his support.

Burr's Conspiracy

The details of Burr's grand plan are still unknown to historians. Some scholars believe that Burr and Wilkinson were planning to take over Texas and establish their own independent nation there. It is certain, however, that Burr never received permission from Jefferson for his Mississippi mission. In 1807, soon after Jackson had withdrawn his support from the expedition, Jefferson had Burr arrested for treason.

Despite his suspicions about Burr's and Wilkinson's intentions, Jackson felt that Burr deserved a fair and honest trial. He appeared at the trial and testified that Burr had never made any treasonous statements in his hearing. There is no doubt that he told the truth. Certainly Jackson's strong sense of honor and patriotism would have prevented him from being involved in treason. But his brief dealings with Burr were later to be used against him by political enemies, who accused him of being part of a seditious conspiracy.

For the present, Jackson found that his association with Burr, innocent though it may have been, had worked against him. His defense of Burr angered President Jefferson, who tried in vain for several years to have Burr convicted. James Madison, who succeeded Jefferson in the presidency, was a great friend of Jefferson and also disliked Jackson because of the Burr affair. As a result, when war broke out with England in 1812 and Jackson eagerly offered his services as a commander, President Madison and his secretary of war did not give him a command. Bitterly opposed to the British since early childhood, Jackson longed to join the fighting, but he was told merely to wait for further orders.

WAR AT SEA AND ON LAND

The War of 1812 was the result of troubles that had been brewing between the United States and England ever since the Revolutionary War ended in 1783. One problem was that the British had not withdrawn from American territory along the Great Lakes as they had agreed to do. To make matters worse, the British continued to encourage Indians to attack American settlers on the frontier. In some cases, the Indians received guns, ammunition, and other supplies from the British in return for their attacks on Americans.

Like other Americans, Jackson was outraged at this support of the Indians against Americans. While it is true that the Indians were fighting for land they had owned for centuries before the settlers arrived, few people of the time were able to sympathize with the Indian point of view. Most Americans, including Jackson, felt it was inevitable that the growth of the United States must push the Indians slowly westward, off the land that would be needed for new farms and towns.

At any rate, Jackson hoped that the United States government would soon take action against the Indians who were causing trouble in the Great Lakes area. One of the worst offenders, from the settlers' point of view, was Tecumseh. He was a Shawnee warrior who urged the various Indian tribes to stop fighting among themselves and unite to battle the American advance into the Northwest Territory. In 1811, Jackson volunteered to lead his militia against Tecumseh, saying that the Indian ought to be "swept off the face of the earth." His offer was not accepted, but later he had many opportunities to fight Indians. Tecumseh took the side of the British when the War of 1812 broke out and was eventually killed in a battle in Canada.

Impressment and Trade

Frontier troubles contributed only partly to the outbreak of war. A still greater cause was England's reluctance to treat its former colony as an independent sovereign state. One way in which the British refused to acknowledge America's independent status involved the practice of impressment, or forcing men into naval service. After years of war with France, the British navy was short of manpower and resorted to desperate means to find sailors. It became quite common for bands of naval agents, called press gangs, to enter British towns and kidnap men and boys, later forcing them to sign into service aboard a navy ship.

Conflict between the United States and England developed when the British, not content with impressing their own men, began forcibly impressing Americans. Sailors who left their ships in British ports ran the risk of being press-ganged in streets or taverns. The British also carried their policy of impressment onto the high seas. British ships ordered American vessels – usually slow, unarmed merchant ships – to halt and be searched. The British claimed to be looking for deserters from the British navy, but they actually seized many American citizens. One dispute between the countries concerned citizenship. England claimed that a British citizen remained a British citizen forever, but the United States allowed people from any country to become naturalized American citizens. As a result, many American sailors who were former British citizens were treated as Englishmen by the seagoing British press-gangs and forcibly taken.

Although the United States government made many official protests against the practice of impressment, press gangs continued to seize American citizens – and sometimes their ships and property, as well. The British refused to discuss the problem, claiming that impressment was their right, and American outrage grew. By 1812, impressment had become a very touchy subject.

While American diplomats were wrestling with the growing problem of impressment, economic issues also propelled the two nations toward war. France and England had been at war intermittently for years, and now each nation tried to keep the United States from engaging in trade with the other. In 1807, England claimed the right to control all shipping to Europe. France retaliated by trying to blockade British ports. At first, the United States responded by cutting off trade with both nations, but this hurt American farmers and merchants, as well as the New England shipping industry. By now some Americans, including the hot-tempered Jackson, were tired of the insults to their country's prestige and the damage to its trade and frontier growth. They began to call for war against England.

Although President Madison had hoped to avoid war, he finally decided he had no choice. The President and Congress declared war in June of 1812. Although Madison had no way of knowing, England had cancelled its crippling trade laws just two days before, as a possible first step toward improved relations between the two countries. The War of 1812 began as it ended, with a time lag in communication. By the time word of the British concession reached the United States, the fighting was underway. The problems between the two nations were expected to be settled on the battlefield.

First Orders and a False Alarm

After his offer to assume a command had been rebuffed, Jackson waited in Tennessee, filled with burning impatience. He followed the war news with the greatest attention. The first fighting was in the North, and dispatches from Detroit and Niagara told of defeats for the Americans. The U.S. War Department suspected that the British would soon attack the South, however, and it was decided that a defense force should proceed to New Orleans. In December of 1812, Jackson received his eagerly awaited marching orders.

He was told to lend his support to Major General Wilkinson, Burr's old ally in the Texas scheme, in the protection of New Orleans. President Madison also hoped that Jackson's men might be useful in an attack on East Florida if the British set up bases in the Spanish-held territory there.

Delighted to be preparing for action at last, Jackson quickly mustered his 2,500 militiamen. Some were cavalrymen, mounted on horses; others were infantry, or foot soldiers. On January 7, 1813, they left Nashville for New Orleans. Although it was winter and travel was hard, they moved fast and covered 1,000 miles in 39 days: down the Cumberland

River to the Ohio River, then down the Ohio to the Mississippi River.

But a disappointment awaited in Natchez, far to the south on the Mississippi. There Jackson received a second set of orders from Secretary of War John Armstrong, telling him to halt in Natchez and await further instructions. He was irritated at the delay, but he did as ordered. When the next set of orders arrived in the middle of March, Jackson read that his services were no longer needed in New Orleans. He was told to disband his men at once.

Old Hickory Earns His Nickname

Jackson had no choice but to accept his orders and return to Nashville, although he was angry that the War Department could not find a use for him when his country was at war. Jackson's response to the orders was typically temperamental: he assumed that someone, perhaps Wilkinson, had arranged the matter to humiliate him. He believed that Wilkinson expected his men to desert and join Wilkinson's own forces.

In reality, however, the decision had little or nothing to do with the individuals involved. Congress had refused to allow a strike against East Florida, and the War Department now felt that New Orleans was safe from attack. So, although he did not know the reasoning behind his orders and resented them greatly, Jackson prepared to obey.

But he refused to disband his men. The federal government had not provided pay, transportation, food, or other supplies for them. Jackson felt that it was his responsibility, as their commander, to see that they got home again. Instead of disbanding, which would have left each man to make his own way home, Jackson led them back to Nashville as a regi-

Clashes between Indians and white settlers punctuated the War of 1812 and Jackson's presidency. His campaign to crush the Creek Indians was kicked off by a massacre of the settlers at Fort Mims in the Mississippi Territory. Here the settlers are shown trying to defend their blazing stockade. (Library of Congress.)

ment. Sick men were given the horses of the cavalrymen and officers. Jackson, too, gave up his horse and walked with his troops all the way home. One of the men, inspired by the 46-year-old Jackson's stamina and determination, said, "He's as tough as old hickory wood." As a result, Jackson returned to Tennessee with a nickname that was to become famous.

THE CAMPAIGN AGAINST THE CREEK INDIANS

Jackson was tremendously disappointed at the outcome of his first venture in the war, but he did not have to wait long for his next call to action. The Creek Indians of the Mississippi Territory had answered Tecumseh's call for Indian unity. They had allied themselves with Tecumseh and the British, and they were attacking settlers in the areas that are now Georgia and Alabama. Called "Red Sticks" because they carried red-dyed war clubs, the Creek were greatly feared.

Late in 1813, Jackson received word that a Creek war party had massacred some 300 white men, women, and children at Fort Mims, an outpost on the Alabama River north of Mobile. Governor Willie Blount of Tennessee called for volunteers to launch a raid against the Creek and authorized Jackson's immediate departure. The major general knew that he would have to move fast to catch the Indian warriors before they slipped into the swamps of Spanish Florida.

Jackson quickly called together 2,000 volunteers, including frontiersmen Davy Crockett and Sam Houston. He marched south to Creek country, through a trackless wilderness. This was the start of a five-month campaign against the Creek. The militia had left Nashville in such great haste that they did not have time to gather sufficient supplies. As a result, the men had to make do with the scanty food and game

William Weatherford, whose Indian name was Red Eagle, was the Creek chief who led the attack on Fort Mims. He is shown surrendering to Jackson after the Battle of Horseshoe Bend. Jackson spared the lives of the remaining Creek. (Library of Congress.)

they found along the way. They also did not have much protection against the cold winter nights. Soon some of the hungry, uncomfortable men began grumbling. On several occasions, Jackson forcibly prevented desertions.

Horseshoe Bend

The Tennessee volunteers fought a number of fierce battles with the Creek over the following months. In March of 1814, they caught up with the main Creek force at a place called Horseshoe Bend in the eastern part of central Alabama. It was the site of the largest Creek village, where the Tallapoosa River formed a U-shaped (horseshoe) bend. The village was located in the bend, protected by the river on three sides. On the fourth side, the Indians had built a log barricade for protection.

Jackson arrayed his forces outside the barricade and offered the Creek a chance to send their women and children across the river to safety before the battle began. Then he attacked. One of Jackson's strengths as a military commander was his ability to use geography to his advantage. At Horseshoe Bend, he sized up the terrain and based his plans on features of the land, just as he was to do later at New Orleans. Jackson realized that the river, which the Indians had used for protection, could also be turned against them. Once the barricade had been stormed by his men, the Indians would be trapped in the U, with no retreat.

The battle went just as Jackson had planned. By the end of the day, he and his men had killed between 800 and 900 Indian warriors—"The carnage was dreadful," Jackson later wrote. They also captured the Creek chief, Red Eagle, who was only one-quarter Indian and whose white name was William Weatherford. It was Weatherford who had led the attack on Fort Mims. He surrendered to Jackson in the hope of saving the lives of the remaining Creek.

A Treaty and a Promotion

Four months later, Jackson called the surviving Creek leaders to a treaty conference at Fort Jackson, a site where Jackson had built a small fort. The treaty, which is known as the Treaty of Fort Jackson, contained harsh peace terms. The Creek were required to give up their claim to about 23 million acres of land in the Mississippi Territory. It gave the United States title to most of present-day Alabama and part of Georgia. By freeing these huge tracts from the Creek threat and opening them to settlement, Jackson became a hero to southerners and westerners alike.

The War Department was impressed by Jackson's decisive victory. Because the War of 1812 was going badly for the United States, the War Department now changed its attitude toward Jackson. It commissioned him a major general in the U.S. Army on May 1, 1814, and appointed him commander of a large military district that included Tennessee, Mississippi, part of Louisiana, and the Southwest Territories. At the time, there was serious danger in the South. The British threatened to seize the Mississippi River at New Orleans and cut off supplies to the American interior.

Jackson moved his army to Mobile, Alabama, in August of 1814. He wanted to keep an eye on affairs in Spanish Florida, because Spain and England were allies in the wars in Europe. Jackson suspected that the Spanish in Florida would support a British invasion of the southern United States.

Attack on Pensacola

In Mobile, Jackson learned that the Spanish settlement at Pensacola, Florida, was being used as a base for British troops preparing to attack Louisiana. He requested permission to attack Pensacola. Time was short and, when word did not arrive from his superiors, Jackson went ahead on his own authority and captured the town in a swift raid on November 7. He discovered in Pensacola that Pakenham's British army had sailed for New Orleans.

Jackson gathered his men and prepared to follow Pakenham, but on land, not by sea. He and his troops left Pensacola on November 22. For the second time in two years, Jackson was marching to the defense of New Orleans. This time, however, there would be no turning back. The War of 1812 would end in little more than a month, and Andrew Jackson, Old Hickory, would be the hero of New Orleans.

Chapter 5

The Road to the Presidency

The Battle of New Orleans, which ended the War of 1812 on a note of victory for the Americans, made Jackson a national hero. After decades as a lawyer and politician, with no military training, he had taken charge of an army at a crucial moment and saved an important city from capture, and possibly from destruction. Not only that, he also had inflicted a stunning defeat on a larger, better-armed force. Old Hickory had indeed proven himself a soldier.

The War Department agreed. It not only asked Jackson to keep his commission as major general in the regular army, it also made him commander of the entire Southern District. Because the war was over, however, he had no real duties in the field. He left the actual command to subordinate officers and returned to The Hermitage. Jackson wanted to get his plantation in order, spend time with Rachel, and regain his health, which had suffered during the long marches of 1814.

Jackson was not allowed to relax for long, however. He had been back in Nashville for only about 2½ months when he received orders from the War Department. Once again he was sent marching south, this time to the border of Spain's territory in Florida. Because Florida had become a grave problem, President Monroe needed Jackson's help.

THE FLORIDA ADVENTURE

The United States had been trying to buy Florida from Spain for many years, but Spain was reluctant to sell. Americans increasingly felt that the entire continent should be open to them, and the presence of an alien force in Florida was irritating to these expansionists. Even more serious, however, was the fact that the Spanish in Florida were beginning to threaten American settlers in Georgia.

The danger came from several sources. The most serious was from Seminole and a few Creek Indians who lived in Florida. They would raid across the border into Georgia, then slip back into Florida. When U.S. troops in Georgia would retaliate with strikes against the Indians, they would respond with more raids and massacres. And so the violence grew. Spain claimed that it did not have enough forts and men in Florida to control the Indians. However, the Americans had reason to believe that the Spanish actually encouraged the Indian raids and provided the Seminole warriors with guns and ammunition.

A Lawless Territory

Spain's poor administration of Florida also made it a haven for some troublemakers who weren't Indians. In 1817, a group of European adventurers tried to form an independent republic on tiny Amelia Island, near the Georgia-Florida border. They launched raids against nearby settlements and also attracted pirates, criminals, and runaway slaves to their island hideout.

Monroe's protests to Spain about the lawless state of the border were ignored. He decided that the United States had no choice but to take action to protect the settlers in Georgia. He also may have hoped that military action along the border would encourage Spain to sell Florida to the United

States. At any rate, Monroe selected Jackson to lead troops to clean up the border area.

It was well known that Jackson believed the United States could and should take Florida by force and argue later with Spain. Jackson's official orders, however, were only to restore order to the border region of Georgia. They did not include any attacks on Spanish posts in Florida. But Jackson was later to claim that he had received other, secret orders from Monroe.

War on the Seminoles

For his own part, Jackson was delighted to be called to service again, especially because he was one of the ardent expansionists who resented any barrier to American settlement in the South and West. He had crushed the Creek resistance, and now he was ready to complete the job by subduing the Seminoles. In December of 1817, he set off at the head of a 2,000-man army. His immediate target was a Seminole war party that had recently killed a boatload of American soldiers.

Jackson was determined to pursue the Indians until he caught them. He finally did catch up with them—in Florida, after chasing them across the border. There he engaged in several battles with the Seminoles. Those Indians who survived were driven deep into the south Florida marshes, where they were no longer a menace to Americans living in Georgia. So vigorous was Jackson's assault on the Seminoles that they gave him the nickname "Sharp Knife."

After his success against the Seminoles, Jackson didn't stop. Perhaps he simply could not pass up the chance to extend American control into Florida. He captured St. Marks, a Spanish fort, claiming that the Spanish there had been giving food and ammunition to the Indians. He then raised the American flag over the fort, manned it with some of his own men, and executed two British subjects he found there. They were an English officer and a Scottish trader who had been teaching the Indians to fight.

Then, for the second time in four years, Jackson took Pensacola. The Spanish in Florida were unable to resist his much larger and stronger force. Within a few months, Jackson had overthrown the Spanish territorial government. He sent the Spanish officials to Cuba and appointed one of his own officers as military governor of the territory.

An International Incident

Unfortunately for Jackson, his invasion of Florida was a case of very poor timing. Just as he was raising the Stars and Stripes over the conquered swamplands, negotiations were finally beginning between Spain and the United States for a peaceful transfer of the territory. But when the Spanish heard of Jackson's invasion, they angrily withdrew from the negotiations. President Monroe feared that Spain would consider the invasion an act of war and perhaps even declare war on the United States.

Having just survived the War of 1812, the United States was not prepared to fight another war. And, as if the possibility of war with Spain were not enough trouble, England protested strongly about what it called the murder of two British civilians. A serious international incident started brewing.

Called upon to explain himself, Jackson claimed that he had received a message from Monroe authorizing him to proceed against the Spanish in Florida, if necessary. But Monroe and Secretary of War John C. Calhoun denied that they had sent such a message. The President's Cabinet considered making formal apologies to Spain and England; Cabinet members even discussed the possibility of taking disciplinary action against Jackson. In the end, however, Secretary of State

John Quincy Adams stood behind Jackson—even though he did not like the major general.

Adams argued that the United States must present a united front to the world and not allow disagreements among its leaders to weaken its position with other nations. Jackson's actions, he said, could be viewed as necessary in the defense of American lives. Adams persuaded Monroe and the Cabinet to support Jackson publicly, although Monroe wrote a private letter to Jackson telling him that he had gone too far in capturing Florida. Jackson replied coldly that he had only been following orders. Adams also wrote a message to Spain, saying that Jackson's invasion had been caused by Spain's failure to control the Indians.

Because of Adams' strong support, Jackson escaped an official reprimand and the possible loss of rank. But Monroe did order the American soldiers to retreat from Florida and then returned the territory to Spain. Less than a year later, however, Spain agreed to sell Florida and some other American land claims to the United States for $5 million. The sale became final in early 1821.

GOVERNOR JACKSON

Once the United States had acquired Florida, President Monroe offered Jackson the opportunity to become the first governor of the new territory. Although Monroe still felt that Jackson had acted wrongly in the invasion of Florida, he knew that the American public was unaware of all the details of the Florida adventure. In the popular mind, Jackson was the conqueror of Florida, and it would have looked ungracious not to offer him the position.

Jackson accepted the post for two reasons. First, he wanted the offer to be seen as a public sign of Monroe's sup-

The Mysterious Mr. Rhea

The full circumstances surrounding Andrew Jackson's invasion of Spanish Florida in early 1818 will probably never be known. Certainly President James Monroe and others in Washington knew of Jackson's firm belief that the Spanish had no place on the American continent. The zealous major general had offered more than once to drive them out of Florida. When he was selected to restore order to the Georgia-Florida border, therefore, the administration in Washington might well have expected him to go further—into Spanish territory itself.

After the deed was done, President Monroe insisted that Jackson had exceeded his orders. Only John Quincy Adams' support prevented a serious international crisis and possible disciplinary measures against Jackson. But Jackson maintained all along that he had only been following orders—special secret orders from the President himself.

Jackson had written to Monroe, suggesting that the United States go ahead and seize Florida by force. He offered to lead the invasion. In reply, Jackson claimed, he had received a message from Monroe, delivered by a man named John Rhea, telling him to proceed with the invasion. Monroe, however, said that he had never replied to Jackson's letter; in fact, he later said that he had not even read it. John Rhea did not come forward to explain himself, and the controversy was allowed to die away.

A few years later, when Jackson was seeking the presidency, he and his friends brought the matter up again. Because they wanted Jackson's name cleared, they sponsored a newspaper campaign to persuade the public that he and Monroe had a secret understanding about the capture of Florida. Monroe denied this, and once again the mysterious John Rhea failed to appear.

In the spring of 1831, the so-called messenger finally came onto the scene. Monroe was ill and dying, and Jackson did not want the former President to die before his own innocence in the Florida business was established. Jackson produced a Tennesseean named John Rhea, who claimed that he had received secret orders from Monroe to be delivered to Jackson in Florida. From his deathbed, the old President made a final denial in a shaking voice. He said he had never seen Rhea in his life. The American people loved Jackson, but they now felt that he had gone too far in harassing the dying Monroe. Jackson let the matter drop, Monroe died, and John Rhea vanished into obscurity.

Did Rhea really carry a message from Monroe to Jackson? Did Jackson really have permission to invade Florida while treaty negotiations with Spain were taking place? No one knows for sure.

port. The question of whether or not Jackson had exceeded his orders in Florida was to haunt him for years. Later, he would make several attempts to prove that he had been in the right. For now, he believed the governorship would show the world that the Florida campaign had been legitimate. Jackson's second reason for accepting the governorship was that he hoped to appoint some of his friends and supporters to positions in the territorial government.

Monroe may have felt that making Jackson governor of Florida was the gracious thing to do, but he also had a more practical reason. Six years earlier, after the Battle of New Orleans, some Americans had begun to say that Old Hickory would make a good President. When Jackson invaded Florida, he had the enthusiastic support of many Americans who wanted to see the last of Spain. These citizens were proud of Jackson's aggressiveness in the national interest and revived the talk of Jackson for President.

Jackson, however, claimed to have no interest in becoming President. In 1821, he responded to rumors of his candidacy with astonishment: "Do they think I am such a damned fool as to think myself fit for President of the United States? I can command a body of men, but I am not fit for President." But many people, supporters as well as opponents, were not so sure of his real feelings. At any rate, because Monroe did not want to see Jackson run for President in 1824, he made him governor of Florida partly to keep him out of the race.

On June 1, 1821, Jackson's military career ended. The 54-year-old soldier resigned his army commission to become the governor of Florida. But Florida seemed to be unlucky for Jackson. His governorship did not go well, and it did not last long. His activities aroused controversy, especially when he threw Jose Callava, the former Spanish governor, into jail for not turning over some official documents to the U.S. administration.

Furthermore, Jackson quickly grew displeased because Monroe ignored most of his recommendations – especially those requesting that Jackson's friends be appointed to government posts. Angry because he felt that his attempt to return to public service was being thwarted by the Monroe administration, Jackson resigned his governorship on December 1, after six months in office. He then returned to Nashville and The Hermitage.

PRESIDENTIAL HOPES

Soon after his return to Tennessee, Jackson did the one thing that Monroe hoped he wouldn't do: he became embroiled in presidential politics. Jackson's entry into the 1824 presidential campaign was at the urging of a powerful group of friends and backers in Tennessee. These men were aware of Jackson's great popularity with the American people. They felt that he could help them achieve their goals and advance himself at the same time. Jackson at first expressed some reluctance, but before long his combination of personal ambition and fervent patriotism kindled his enthusiasm for the idea.

Jackson's involvement in the campaign grew out of a plan to turn his fame to the advantage of a group of local politicians headed by John Overton, Jackson's old friend from the days of Mrs. Donelson's boardinghouse. Overton and his friends wanted to announce Jackson as a presidential candidate and attach one of their number, a man named Pleasant Miller, to him as a senatorial candidate. Jackson's popularity would give Miller the boost he needed to be elected to the Senate, and then Jackson's presidential campaign could be left to die away.

The first stages of the campaign went according to plan. In 1822, the Tennessee legislature nominated Jackson for the presidency. But the popular response was even greater than Jackson's backers had expected. All sections of the nation greeted Jackson's candidacy with immediate and strong support. Seeing this, the political faction that had brought about the nomination lost interest in Pleasant Miller and began to take Jackson's prospects seriously.

Steps to the Senate

It seemed to Jackson's political cronies that he could not be elected President without having held an elected office since his brief service in the Senate in 1797. Led by two of Jackson's closest advisors, William B. Lewis and John H. Eaton, this faction managed to persuade the Tennessee legislature to make Jackson a candidate for the senatorial position that Miller had hoped to win. At that point in Tennessee's history, the senatorial election was something of a formality once the candidate had received the legislature's approval. Jackson therefore won the election easily. In November of 1823, he returned to the U.S. Senate after an absence of 25 years.

"I am a senator against my wishes and feelings," Jackson said at one point, clearly indicating that he had no real interest in the post. But his advisors persuaded him that it was essential for anyone who hoped to become President to have a seat in Congress. In the meantime, Monroe was not pleased to see Jackson in Washington, D.C., obviously grooming himself for the President's House, as the White House was then called. Monroe offered Jackson a desirable post, the ambassadorship to Mexico, hoping to lure the Tennessean out of the presidential race. Jackson declined, however, making his presidential goal unmistakably clear. He was a serious candidate for the 1824 election—and an extremely popular one.

Party Politics

At this time, the United States had only one effective political party. A two-party system had arisen during the administration of John Adams, the second President. But the Federalist party had steadily lost strength over the years and virtually ceased to exist after the War of 1812. The remaining party was known as the Democratic-Republican Party. It was far from united, however, as many groups and factions within the party disagreed with one another.

The Democratic-Republicans were unable to agree on a single presidential candidate. A caucus, or committee, in Congress chose William H. Crawford of Georgia, Monroe's secretary of the treasury, as its candidate. But local party organizations and state legislatures added rival candidates, some of them the most accomplished and respected political figures of the time: Secretary of State John Quincy Adams of Massachusetts, the son of former President John Adams; Henry Clay of Kentucky, who was the Speaker of the House of Representatives and extremely popular in the West; John C. Calhoun of South Carolina, who had served as secretary of war under Monroe; and, of course, Andrew Jackson, the hero of New Orleans and the great Indian fighter.

Jackson was no longer the rowdy, unpolished frontiersman who had felt out of place in eastern society back in the 1790s. He was now a dignified country gentleman who presented a soldierly appearance. A bit over six feet tall, Jackson was, at 150 pounds, as lean and trim as a young man. His eyes were still a snapping clear blue, and his thick gray hair swept impressively back from his forehead. He often wore an officer's cape, and he carried himself ramrod-straight. Representative Daniel Webster of Massachusetts said in 1824 that Jackson's manners were "more presidential" than those of the other candidates.

Before long, Calhoun dropped out of the presidential race, satisfied with the prospect of becoming Vice-President. Then Crawford suffered a serious stroke. He refused to withdraw his candidacy, but everyone realized that he was no longer likely to win.

The Vote of 1824

When the American people and the electoral college voted in the fall of 1824, both the popular and electoral votes were indecisive. No candidate received a majority of the votes — that is, a number greater than the total received by all the other candidates. But Jackson and his supporters were thrilled to see that he had received a plurality of popular and electoral votes — in other words, he had received the most votes, but not more than half of the total.

Jackson received 155,800 popular votes; Adams, 105,300; Clay, 46,500; and Crawford, 44,200. Because the electoral college really elected the President, the electoral vote was considered more important than the popular vote. Here again Jackson led, with 99 votes to Adams' 84, Crawford's 41, and Clay's 37.

At the time, if an electoral vote failed to produce a majority, the House of Representatives elected the President from among the three candidates with the highest number of electoral votes. This meant that Clay, with the lowest number, was out of the race. As Speaker of the House, however, he wielded enormous power over the outcome of the vote, because many congressmen were influenced by his opinions. And because Crawford was too ill to serve as President, the race was now clearly between Adams and Jackson.

The "Corrupt Bargain"

It was known that Clay opposed Jackson's candidacy, partly because he felt the Tennesseean was too inexperienced for the job and partly because he was jealous of Jackson's immense popularity among westerners. Whatever his motives, Clay gave his support to Adams. When the House voted, Adams won the votes of 13 states; Jackson, seven; and Crawford, four. John Quincy Adams had been elected the sixth President of the United States.

At first, Jackson accepted his defeat with good grace. Then he learned that the new President planned to appoint Clay to the post of secretary of state. This was the most highly prized and desirable post in the Cabinet, because the secretary of state commonly became the next President.

When he heard this news, Jackson and his followers were convinced that Adams and Clay had struck what they called a "corrupt bargain": Clay's support of Adams in the House vote in return for Clay getting the Cabinet post. Jackson's scorn for Clay was evident when he said, in an indignant outburst, "So you see, the Judas of the West has closed his contract and will receive the 30 pieces of silver."

This was the beginning of a long and bitter rivalry between Jackson on one side and Adams and Clay on the other. Even though Adams had supported Jackson in the matter of the Florida invasion, the diplomat from Massachusetts had no liking for the lawyer from Tennessee, nor did he try to hide his feelings. He described Jackson as "incompetent both by his ignorance and by the fury of his passions." And Clay said of Jackson, "I cannot believe that the killing of 2,000 Englishmen at New Orleans . . . qualifies a person for the presidency." Jackson was equally blunt, calling Clay "the basest, meanest scoundrel that ever disgraced the image of God."

THE BIRTH OF JACKSONIAN DEMOCRACY

The election of 1824, and the accusations of a deal between Adams and Clay, aroused nationwide interest and passion. People who had voted for Jackson were proud that he had won the most votes—and angry that he was not to be their next President. They felt that the people's choice had been blocked by a group of professional politicians. Jackson agreed. He was bitter over his defeat, but he was also determined to succeed in the 1828 election.

Jackson resigned from the Senate in 1825. He was unwilling to serve under the Adams administration, and he wanted to return to private life. He also felt that he could best develop his next presidential campaign on home ground in Tennessee. And he knew, from the large number of votes he had received in 1824, that he did not have to prove himself a dedicated public servant to the American people.

Over the next few years, Jackson and his supporters built a highly effective political organization. They drew upon the growing political interests of the common people: farmers, urban factory and office workers, shopowners, and small businessmen. They also assured western frontiersmen and southern planters that Jackson would look after them better than the old-line eastern politicians. The spokesmen for this Jacksonian movement were vigorous newspaper editors like Isaac Hill and Duff Green, who knew that a Jackson presidency would bring wide-ranging social changes. Such men felt that these changes would be both profitable and beneficial to the nation.

Major changes in the nature of American voters took place in the years leading up to the election of 1828. These changes helped bring about the rise of Jacksonian democracy—that is, emphasis on the importance of the individual American, rather than on established parties or families, in shaping the destiny of the nation. Before 1828, voters had to meet certain requirements of property ownership. The states removed these requirements between 1800 and 1828, however, making sharecroppers, factory workers, and small farmers eligible to vote for the first time. In addition, the admission of new states to the Union greatly increased the number of southern and western voters, who were likely to share the spirit of Jacksonian democracy. Although women had not yet won the right to vote, the election of 1828 promised to be the most democratic election yet held in the United States.

Jackson's Allies and Opponents

One of the strengths of Jackson's presidential campaign was the assistance of Senator Martin Van Buren of New York. Short, plump, and red-haired, Van Buren was sometimes called the "Red Fox" or the "Little Magician" in tribute to his political cunning. He had supported Crawford in 1824, but Crawford's retirement due to illness brought Van Buren into Jackson's camp.

As a supporter of Crawford, Van Buren had acquired a following among voters and politicians in Virginia and Georgia. He encouraged these and other southerners to rally behind Jackson. Van Buren and Calhoun, Adams' Vice-President, were the most prominent of Jackson's supporters (at that time it was possible for a President and Vice-President to belong to different parties). With Van Buren as Jackson's campaign manager, a new political party began to form around Old Hickory.

The Democratic-Republican Party was permanently split. President Adams, Clay, and their followers now called themselves the National Republicans. Their candidate was Adams, hoping for re-election; his secretary of the treasury,

Richard Rush, was the vice-presidential candidate. The National Republican Party absorbed the few remaining members of the old Federalist Party. A few years later, the National Republican Party changed its name to the Whig Party.

Jackson and his supporters continued to call themselves the Democratic-Republicans, but many soon began to shorten the name to Democrats. Historians trace the origin of the modern Democratic Party to this Jacksonian group within the Democratic-Republicans.

Freemasons and Anti-Masons

For the first time, a third party appeared in American politics. Formed in 1827, it was called the Anti-Masonic Party. The Anti-Masons wanted to combat the influence of the Order of Freemasons, a fraternal lodge to which Jackson and many other politicians of the time belonged. The Masonic Order was very old, with roots that reached back for centuries into European history. Nonmembers periodically accused it of having secret political power or of some other evil machinations.

In 1826, a New Yorker named William Morgan, who had written a book claiming to prove that the Masons were up to no good, disappeared. He was believed to have been murdered. Suspicion of the Masons briefly gained strength, and the incident sparked the founding of the Anti-Masonic Party. The party played little part in the election of 1828, however, and within a decade it had merged with the Whigs.

A BRUTAL CAMPAIGN

The election of 1828 was one of the hardest fought contests in the history of American politics. It introduced much of what 20th-century Americans recognize as an accepted part of a presidential campaign: slogans, rallies, buttons, banners, souvenirs, and other items and activities designed to promote individual candidates and get people involved in the race. Quite a bit of this presidential hoopla was the work of Van Buren, who eagerly seized upon new campaign strategies and used them to the fullest. He stressed Jackson's military accomplishments, losing no opportunity to remind the public that Jackson was the hero of New Orleans, the conqueror of Florida, and the defender of the frontier against the Indians.

The 1828 election quickly became notable for something else as well: the extraordinary number of personal insults and slanders that were pronounced by both sides. Most historians agree that it was the meanest, most malicious presidential campaign ever. Most of the mudslinging, however, was carried out not by the candidates themselves but by speechmakers and newspaper editors who supported them.

Adams' supporters tried to diminish Jackson's military prestige by digging up or manufacturing unsavory incidents in his command. One handbill that was widely circulated showed six black coffins and accused Jackson of having murdered six good soldiers; in reality, the men were deserters whom Jackson had ordered executed. The anti-Jacksonians also brought up the old matter of the Jacksons' irregular marriage, and the ugly name-calling greatly distressed Rachel Jackson.

Jackson's backers were just as guilty. They accused Adams of all sorts of secret vices, from gambling in the President's House to supplying women to the tsar (emperor) of Russia (Adams had served as ambassador to Russia early in his career). One of Jackson's campaign posters used a children's nursery rhyme, "The House that Jack Built," to describe Adams and his Cabinet members as rats who were infesting the President's House.

The campaign of 1828 was probably the meanest and hardest-fought presidential campaign in American history. Jackson's opponents tried to smear his reputation with this coffin-covered handbill, which accused him of murdering six American soldiers during the War of 1812. In reality, the men were deserters who were executed according to military law. (Library of Congress.)

Victory and Tragedy

The result of all this personal abuse was that the voters paid far less attention to national issues and to the qualifications of the candidates than to the insults they leveled at one another. But the outcome was never in doubt. When the votes were counted in November of 1828, Jackson had won 648,273 popular votes against Adams' 508,064. Jackson's edge was even greater in the all-important electoral vote, which was 178 to 83. John Quincy Adams lost his chance to serve for a second term, and Andrew Jackson became the seventh President of the United States.

Jackson's victory may be called the first true democratic election of a President. Up until this time, the electors of many states were appointed by the governor or the state legislature. This meant that the electors did not always vote in a way that reflected the will of the people. But by 1828, all states except Delaware and South Carolina chose their electors by popular vote. It was also the first election in which the candidates were nominated by state legislatures and popular rallies, rather than by caucuses of congressmen. Jackson had both inspired and benefited from this trend toward a more universal form of American democracy.

The President-elect's elation over his victory was soon shattered by a personal tragedy. For years, Rachel Jackson had led a quiet, private life. She spent most of her time at home, where she kept busy overseeing the house, reading her Bible, and visiting with friends. During these years her health gradually declined, and it grew worse under the stress of the 1828 presidential campaign—especially her unhappiness at seeing pamphlets and articles raking up the old scandal of her bigamous marriage. Not long after her husband's victory at the polls, Rachel had a heart attack. She died on December 22, 1828, and was buried at The Hermitage on Christmas Eve.

Jackson was stricken by grief and anger, believing that the lies of his political opponents had caused Rachel's death. But he did not have much time to remain at home with his sorrow—his new job was waiting for him. In January of 1829, he set off for Washington, accompanied by a few friends and by his nephew, Andrew Jackson Donelson, who was to be his private secretary. Although he was on his way to the presidency, Jackson expected the President's House to be a lonely place. After 37 years of marriage, he could no longer cheer himself with the thought of Rachel waiting for him at home.

Chapter 6

The People's President

C rowds of cheering admirers lined the streets of every community to applaud Jackson on his way from Nashville to Washington. He was pleased by the people's display of excitement and good feeling, and the sadness caused by his wife's death began to lift. He even mounted the driver's seat of his carriage to address the crowds on several occasions. By the time Jackson arrived in Washington on February 11, 1829, he was over the worst of his grief and was looking forward to the challenges of the presidency.

Jackson was inaugurated on March 4. It was warm and sunny, a fine day for an inauguration. The oath of office was administered on the porch of the President's House by Chief Justice John Marshall. A salute of cannon fire honored the new President. Then Jackson walked to the Capitol, followed by a huge crowd of well-wishers, ranging from dignified statesmen to rugged frontiersmen and veterans of the Revolutionary War. John Quincy Adams, the outgoing President, was conspicuously absent. Like his father, who had refused to attend the inauguration of his successor, Thomas Jefferson, Adams did not attend Jackson's inauguration.

Jackson addressed the crowd. He was suffering from

This painting appears on the ceiling of the Capitol building in Washington, D.C. Jackson is shown receiving the presidential oath of office from Chief Justice John Marshall on March 4, 1829. The man at the lower right wears the uniform of a veteran of the American Revolution.

tuberculosis and other ailments, and his speech was punctuated by spasms of coughing. Nevertheless, his blue eyes sparkled brightly from a face drawn thin and lined with illness. "The Federal Constitution must be obeyed, state rights preserved, our national debt must be paid, direct taxes and loans avoided, and the Federal Union preserved," Jackson told his followers. "These are the objects I have in view, and regardless of all consequence will carry into effect."

"King Mob"

The crowds rushed forward to shake Jackson's hand. Ten thousand people had swarmed into Washington—a city whose population was only 18,000—to attend the inauguration. A tremendous sense of excitement and anticipation filled the air. Jackson, the ordinary people felt, was *their* President, and many thousands of them descended on the President's House, where Jackson had planned to greet the public informally.

Because he was still in mourning for Rachel, Jackson had refused to allow any formal celebrations, but he felt that it would be a good idea to have a sort of open house for his friends and supporters. No one could have foreseen what was going to happen at the President's House on that day.

Hordes of happy Jacksonians poured into the rooms and rushed at the food that had been prepared for the reception: cake, orange punch, and ice cream. The crowds broke dishes and glasses, damaged furniture and dirtied rugs, smashed windows, and even shoved the President aside. In fact, Jackson was so dismayed by the melee that he escaped through a window and retreated to Gadsby's Hotel, where he had often stayed when he visited Washington. Meanwhile, the waiters at the President's House finally lured the crowd outside by removing the food and punch to the lawn.

Nothing like this riotous display had ever been seen in Washington. One observer called it "The Reign of King Mob." And some conservatives, people who were disturbed by the idea of power in the hands of the unpredictable masses, believed that the disgraceful event was an omen of disaster to come under Jackson's administration. But many people felt the celebration proved that Jackson recognized the rights and importance of the common people. It was a symbol of his connection to what has come to be called the grass roots of American politics: everyday men and women.

THE FIRST TERM

Jackson entered the presidency without any clear program or political philosophy. Not since Washington, the first President, had the nation been led by someone who had not spent many years gaining experience in government service and foreign policy. But Jackson possessed personal qualities that were to make him a vigorous and firm President.

Jackson's bravery and devotion to his country were unquestioned. His career as a judge had shown that he was not afraid to form opinions and act on them. And his military career demonstrated his ability to analyze problems as they came up and take whatever action was needed to solve them.

These are the qualities that Jackson demonstrated throughout his eight years as President. He was a strong-willed leader who kept the reins of power firmly in his own hands. In fact, he was so decisive and so determined to remain in full control of the government that his opponents took to criticizing his masterful leadership by calling him "King Andrew I." But Jackson continued to do pretty much what he wanted as President, in the firm belief that it was what the majority of the people wanted, too.

BORN TO COMMAND.

OF VETO MEMORY.

HAD I BEEN CONSULTED.

KING ANDREW THE FIRST.

Jackson's critics accused him of tyrannical, even dictatorial, government. This early political caricature shows "King Andrew the First" dressed like a member of the hated European monarchy, trampling on the Constitution. (Library of Congress.)

The Victor and the Spoils

Jackson's administration has come to be associated with a practice called the spoils system, from the saying "To the victor belongs the spoils" (spoils are the prizes of war). Under the spoils system, political appointments are given by those in power to friends or to people who have done favors for them. This practice, also known as patronage, was an accepted reality of political life long before Jackson was elected. But because he and his party had announced that they planned to make major changes in the administration, Jackson had no sooner arrived in Washington than he was beseiged with people seeking appointments or federal jobs.

Because many of these office-seekers were rewarded, Jackson's critics later claimed that he had weakened the administration by removing nearly all experienced officeholders and replacing them with his friends. But that was not true. In two terms as President, Jackson removed only 250 of 600 high-ranking appointees and about 900 of 10,000 civil servants—less than one-tenth of the total number of federal officeholders.

Jackson believed that he was doing more than just rewarding friends and supporters by giving them appointments and jobs. He felt that federal offices should not be monopolized by wealthy people or families, or by long-established bureaucrats. He feared that such a system would lead to the creation of a permanent aristocracy like that of England. Jackson declared that no federal employee should consider holding office to be a lifetime right. He also said that the system of replacing workers made the government more democratic by giving more people a chance to work for it.

Two Presidential Cabinets

One of Jackson's first activities as President was to name the members of his Cabinet, the appointed officials who are responsible for various government departments. In return for his support in the campaign, John C. Calhoun had been given the vice-presidency. To the important post of secretary of state, Jackson appointed his close advisor, Martin Van Buren. Another good friend, John H. Eaton, was made secretary of war; Eaton was a Tennesseean who had been one of Jackson's early backers in the 1824 campaign. Jackson then allowed Calhoun to appoint the remainder of the Cabinet: Samuel D. Ingham as secretary of the treasury; John M. Berrien as attorney general; William T. Berry as postmaster general; and John Branch as secretary of the navy.

Unfortunately, Jackson's first term was dominated by a contest between Van Buren and Calhoun to become Jackson's likely successor in the next election, as both men believed Jackson would be too ill to run again. Van Buren marshalled support by gathering a group of advisors around himself and Jackson. Because these men held no official Cabinet posts, they were sometimes called the "Kitchen Cabinet"– informal counselors who would meet with Jackson almost daily in the back rooms of the President's House to discuss the affairs of government. Among them were Francis Blair, editor of the pro-Jackson Washington *Globe*; Duff Green, editor of the *United States Telegraph*, a newspaper that initially supported Jackson but later switched its support to Calhoun; Andrew Jackson Donelson, the President's nephew by marriage and his private secretary; Isaac Hill, formerly a newspaper editor and now a senator from New Hampshire; and Roger Brooke Taney, who in 1836 was named Chief Justice of the U.S. Supreme Court by Jackson and was the first Catholic to hold that post.

Central Government vs. States' Rights

One issue that created a rift between Jackson and Calhoun was the question of states' rights, which was developing into one of the most pressing and perplexing political problems of the age. How much control did the federal government have over the states? How much freedom did the states have to act independently? Because these questions were not fully answered by the Constitution, they had to be worked out in a series of decisions over the years. Some people favored a strong federal government, while others favored a high degree of independence for the states, or states' rights. The issue was one that sharply divided politicians for many years.

The nature of the union that bound the states together was still being explored in the 19th century. Colonial Americans, wary of a strong centralized rule because of their experiences under the British monarchy, had built up a tradition of local self-rule through such structures as town meetings and town councils. Because this tradition continued, many people demanded a clear definition of the rights and limitations of larger ruling bodies, such as the federal government.

Some leaders, including Thomas Jefferson, had followed a strict interpretation of the issue; they allowed the central government only those rights that are specifically granted to it in the Constitution. Others, following the so-called federalist interpretation of Alexander Hamilton, had believed in a stronger, more centralized federal government, with the power to do anything that was not specifically ruled out by the Constitution. Sooner or later, every politician or statesman of Jackson's time had to take a stand on this issue.

Jackson had been known to lean slightly in the direction of states' rights, but he also felt that the union of the states must be protected at all costs. Between 1828 and 1830, Calhoun brought about a crisis that forced Jackson to take a stand against states' rights.

Like Jackson, Calhoun had initially leaned toward states' rights. But his growing desire to distance himself from the President in his political views, combined with developments in his home state of South Carolina, made Calhoun come out forcefully in favor of a state's right to independent action. South Carolina was disturbed by tariffs (taxes on imported goods and products) that were intended to keep the cost of imports high. This ensured a good market—and high prices—for locally produced goods. The manufacturers of the New England states benefited from these tariffs, but the farmers of the South and West resented the higher prices they caused. In addition, many southerners feared that a strong federal government could threaten their slave-holding rights. Slaves, they believed, were vital to the plantation economy of the South.

At the request of his state's legislature, Calhoun wrote a resolution claiming that the state could nullify, or cancel, any federal act that it felt to be unconstitutional. This nullification paper, as it came to be known, was officially anonymous—that is, the name of the author was not revealed—but everyone knew that it had been written by Calhoun. In the opinion of Jackson, Van Buren, and other members of the Kitchen Cabinet, the nullification theory presented a serious threat to the Union.

Van Buren and his supporters in the President's circle, hoping to widen the rift between Jackson and Calhoun, maneuvered the President into making a toast in favor of a strong central government at an important political event, the Jefferson Day dinner on April 13, 1830. "Our Federal Union!" he announced as he raised his glass. "It must be preserved!" To which Calhoun responded, "The Union, next

When elected President for his first term, Jackson's Vice-President was John C. Calhoun of South Carolina. However, after their relationship became a stormy one because of many disagreements, Jackson did not name Calhoun as his running mate for his second term. (Library of Congress.)

to our liberty, most dear." The positions of the two men had been spelled out: Jackson was defending the federal government, and Calhoun was claiming that the liberties of individual states could not be threatened.

To make matters even worse between the two men, Jackson now discovered that Calhoun had been highly critical of his Florida campaign in 1818. Calhoun, who had been secretary of war at the time, had even recommended that Jackson be punished for invading Florida. When Jackson demanded an explanation from his Vice-President, Calhoun made a tactical error. He published some documents about the Florida adventure in a newspaper and brought the 12-year-old controversy into the public eye once more. Jackson was furious and thoroughly fed up with his Vice-President.

The Barmaid and the President

The rivalry between Calhoun and Van Buren followed a winding course. At one time, in the so-called "Eaton Affair," it even had Washington's hostesses battling. Secretary of War John Eaton had married a vivacious barmaid named Peggy O'Neale. She was the widow of a navy man. Rumors soon circulated, probably started by Calhoun, that Peggy's husband had killed himself because of his wife's involvement with Eaton. Calhoun's wife refused to socialize with the new Mrs. Eaton, and the other Cabinet wives and Washington hostesses followed her lead.

Jackson was furious at this cruel treatment of his friend's wife. It reminded him of the social difficulties he and Rachel had faced. He staunchly defended Mrs. Eaton. He became so angry that he actually called a special meeting of the Cabinet to interview Peggy Eaton and judge her social acceptability.

As might have been expected, this surprising move not only did not produce the desired results, it also brought renewed ridicule in the press. Some friends urged Jackson to remove Eaton from his Cabinet, but Old Hickory's strong sense of personal loyalty was outraged. "I would resign the presidency," he said, "sooner than desert my friend Eaton." Only Van Buren, who had no wife to object to Peggy's presence, remained friendly with the Eatons. This endeared Van Buren to the President.

The Eaton affair was most likely a scheme of Calhoun's that backfired. Calhoun expected Eaton to resign in order to avoid scandal, and he thought Van Buren would be forced to resign as a gesture of support. This finally happened in 1831. Unfortunately for Calhoun, however, the affair left both Eaton and Van Buren deeper than ever in the President's good graces. Eaton was awarded the governorship of Florida and, later, the post of ambassador to Spain. And when Jackson announced that he would run for a second term in 1832, he said that Van Buren would be his running mate.

Clay, Calhoun, and the "Force Bill"

The states' rights issue continued to plague Jackson in 1832, his fourth year in office. Once again, South Carolina was the source of the trouble. This time, however, Henry Clay, Jackson's enemy since the 1824 election, entered the picture.

Clay, the congressman from Kentucky, was a firm believer in spending federal money on projects within the individual states. He especially wanted federal funds to build a section of the so-called National Road between Maysville and Lexington in Kentucky. Clay argued that this road, the nation's first major highway, would improve trade between East and West and thus benefit the whole nation. But in 1830

Jackson vetoed the Maysville Bill, which would have provided federal funds for the project, saying that the road was of greatest benefit to Kentucky and therefore Kentucky should pay for it. This deepened the division between Clay and Jackson. But the President's political actions were not always consistent. His administration actually increased overall federal spending for such internal improvements as roads, canals, and harbors in various states.

Surprisingly, Clay and Jackson found themselves on the same side of an issue in 1832. South Carolina was still simmering over the tariff problem when Clay wrote a compromise bill that lowered some of the taxes that had been imposed by a previous tariff bill. Clay and Jackson hoped that the new bill would soothe the irate southerners.

Their hopes were not realized, however. The southerners were angry that the high tariffs on some goods essential to plantation farming—iron and rope, for example—had been kept. At Calhoun's urging, South Carolina acted upon Calhoun's "nullification" resolution and declared that the new federal tariffs did not apply in South Carolina. The state threatened to secede from the Union if it were forced to obey the tariff. Some people felt that civil war was just around the corner. It was the most serious threat the Union had yet faced.

Jackson could not permit the federal government to give in to such a threat, nor could he permit the Union to be broken. He sent troops to South Carolina in a clear demonstration that he was willing to use armed force, if necessary, to enforce the law. He also addressed a proclamation to the people of the state, warning them that they were on the verge of treason.

Because Jackson did not want to use force against his native state, he asked Clay to write another compromise tariff bill. This time Calhoun and his supporters agreed to Clay's proposals. At the same time, however, Jackson signed into law a bill called the "Force Bill," which authorized him to use the U.S. Army and Navy if necessary to collect taxes and tariff duties. But the crisis was averted and the issue resolved when South Carolina repealed Calhoun's nullification act. Angry and humiliated, Calhoun resigned as Vice-President; the term was almost over, anyway. He later went on to become a senator from South Carolina.

The Indian Issue

Jackson's decisions sometimes surprised his friends and enemies alike. His practice was to evaluate each issue separately as it arose, rather than to state broad policies that would cover a number of individual issues. As a result, his actions could appear inconsistent. For example, although he had stood firm on the side of the federal government against states' rights in the case of South Carolina and the tariff issue, he came out on the side of states' rights in the case of Georgia and the Cherokee Indians. It was one of several Indian issues that were among the most troublesome problems of Jackson's presidency.

After gold was discovered on the tribal lands of the Cherokees in northwest Georgia, the state wanted to claim about nine million acres of this land. The Indians, however, held title to the land under a treaty with the federal government that had been made in 1802. Georgia asked the federal government to remove the Indians from the land, then the state tried to buy the land from the Indians. Both attempts failed. Now, in 1829, the state began confiscating the land and removing the Indians by force.

The Indians sought assistance from missionary societies in New England. With the help of humanitarian and church groups, the Indians won two favorable decisions in the Supreme Court; both decisions were handed down by Chief Justice John Marshall, whom Jackson disliked. But Georgia defied the Supreme Court's orders. When the Court turned to Jackson for enforcement, he refused to send federal troops into Georgia. He is said to have remarked, "Well, John Marshall has made his decision, now let him enforce it." Then, in 1830, Congress passed the Indian Removal Act. This act required Indians in the settled part of the country to turn over their lands to the federal government upon request. Although the act also required that the Indians be paid for their property and given new homes in the territories west of the Mississippi River, it failed utterly to consider the Indian point of view.

Because of the Indian Removal Act and the failure to enforce the Supreme Court orders protecting the Cherokees in Georgia, Jackson is often thought of as a bitter enemy of the Indians. But the truth is not so simple.

Jackson had fought harsh wars against the Creek and Seminole Indians, but he was not an Indian-hater. Like nearly all Americans of the time, he believed, however, that the Indians must inevitably give way to the whites as their settlements encroached on Indian territories. Because the Indians were greatly outnumbered by the whites, many observers felt that their way of life was doomed.

By removing the Indians from settled states to unsettled territories, Jackson felt that he was giving most Americans what they wanted. He was also giving the Indians an opportunity to live unmolested in a region where they would not be killed by settlers or militia. The failure of the whites to recognize and respect the Indians' rights is a sad and shameful chapter in American history, but Jackson was no more guilty than most other Americans of his day.

As for the Cherokees of Georgia, they refused to submit peacefully to the Indian Removal Act. Finally, in 1838, during the adminstration of Jackson's successor, Martin Van Buren, they were forced off their land by Georgia militiamen and sent to Arkansas, 800 miles from their homes. Many died during this sad march, which later became known as the "Trail of Tears." Eventually, the remaining Cherokees settled in the Oklahoma Territory.

Chapter 7

The Reign of King Andrew

As the end of his first term in office drew near, Jackson made it clear that he would run again. It also seemed clear to everyone that he would win the election quite easily. His opponents, notably Henry Clay and Daniel Webster, decided to make it more difficult for him. In 1832, as the elections approached, they introduced a problem that dominated Jackson's second term in office: the Bank of the United States, which Jackson later called "a monster."

Jackson's philosophy of banking and money was quite simple: he was dedicated to "hard money"–that is, to gold and silver. Early in his career, when he was speculating in land, he lost a great deal of money when promissory notes issued by local banks turned out to be worthless. Because of this experience, he distrusted paper currency forever afterward.

Clay and other anti-Jacksonians knew that the President and many of the people who had voted for him distrusted the Bank of the United States. Therefore, although the bank's charter (permission from the government to operate) was not due to be renewed until 1836, Clay and the bank's president, a Philadelphian named Nicholas Biddle, rushed through Congress a bill to recharter the bank.

This placed Jackson in a dilemma. He could either sign the bill and renew the charter, which would displease many voters, or he could veto the bill and refuse to renew the charter, which would displease business interests and the bank's powerful friends in Congress.

THE BATTLE OF THE BANK

The Bank of the United States was not a government institution. Instead, it was a private corporation. The federal government owned one-fifth of the bank's stock and used the bank for federal banking needs. The Bank of the United States had no legal power, but its advice guided the government in regulating state and local banks.

The bank had a good record in handling public funds and keeping the national currency stable. But Jackson and some others felt that the bank was more devoted to the interests of a few moneyed easterners—mostly its stockholders—than to those of the nation at large. As the bank was, in fact, a private business, this was probably correct. Jackson did not want a private business to have so much power in the government and to control the investment of federal funds. As early as his first annual message to Congress, in 1829, he had warned that he had doubts about rechartering the bank.

A Presidential Veto

When the recharter bill came before Jackson in 1832 for his approval, he and his Cabinet agreed that he should veto it. Jackson was particularly indignant because the move to renew the charter long before necessary was an obvious ploy to put pressure on him during an election year. He was ill and temporarily confined to his bed at the time, but his energy was unimpaired. When Van Buren went to visit Jackson, the President vowed from his sickbed, "The bank, Mr. Van Buren, is trying to kill me, but I will kill it!"

Jackson did more than just veto the recharter bill. He attacked the bank in a 7,000-word veto message that was delivered to Congress in July of 1832. In his message, Jackson acknowledged that a national bank would be a good thing, if it were properly organized and run. But he accused the Bank of the United States of being a monopoly that benefited "the richest class" of Americans at the expense of "the earnings of the American people." The message closed with a reminder that "the rich and powerful often bend the acts of government to their selfish purpose."

This stirring message appealed to the ordinary working-class people who were the backbone of Jacksonian democracy. Biddle, the bank's president, dismissed it as a "manifesto of anarchy." But it was clear that he and the Bank of the United States would have a battle on their hands when the bank needed to be rechartered in 1836.

THE ELECTION OF 1832

The election of 1832 was the first in which a presidential candidate was nominated by a convention of representatives from the entire nation. It was thus the beginning of the present-day custom of national conventions.

The first national convention took place in Baltimore, Maryland, in May of 1832, and nominated Andrew Jackson as the official presidential candidate of the Democratic-Republican party. Of course, Jackson's nomination had been taken for granted. But the convention also confirmed Jackson's choice of Martin Van Buren as the party's vice-presidential candidate. Van Buren easily won the nomination by 208 of 283 possible votes.

The official name of Jackson's party at this time was the Republican Party, but no one called it that. It was usually called the Democratic-Republican Party, or simply the Democratic Party. Eight years later, at the 1840 national convention, the party formally changed its name to the Democratic Party, the direct ancestor of today's Democrats. The party is therefore one of the oldest surviving political organizations in the world.

The National Republicans, the opposition party, nominated Henry Clay as its presidential candidate and John Sergeant of Pennsylvania, an officer of the Bank of the United States, for Vice-President. The Anti-Masonic Party held a convention and nominated candidates, but they were not considered serious contenders. A fourth group, called the Independent Party, also appeared in the election. This party consisted only of a few discontented South Carolinians who still wanted to uphold the principle of nullification. By the 1836 election, the National Republicans, Anti-Masonics, and Independents had merged to form the Whig Party.

The election was an easy win for Jackson. He received 687,502 popular votes, as opposed to Clay's 530,189. The electoral vote was even more firmly on Jackson's side: 219 to Clay's 49. It appeared to most observers that Jackson won not because the voters were agitated about the bank issue but because of the great affection they felt for him. One defeated National Republican commented, "My opinion is that he [Jackson] may be President for life if he chooses."

Jackson Firsts

Andrew Jackson was the first United States President:

- who was born in a log cabin.
- who was born west of the Allegheny Mountains.
- who was born in South Carolina.
- who was a resident of a state other than the one he had been born in.
- who was nominated as a candidate by a national party convention.
- who received a plurality of the popular vote but did not win the election (in 1824).
- who was the target of an assassination attempt.
- who rode a railroad train (in 1833; John Quincy Adams had ridden the same train several months earlier, but he was no longer President).
- who signed a formal presidential protest against a congressional resolution (in 1834 the Senate resolved that Jackson had exceeded his powers in a tax decision).
- who appointed a Catholic as Chief Justice of the Supreme Court (Roger Brooke Taney, in 1836).

THE SECOND TERM

During his second term, Jackson appointed new men to replace the Cabinet that had been disrupted by the maneuvers of Calhoun and Van Buren during the previous term. Louis

GENERAL JACKSON SLAYING THE MANY HEADED MONSTER.

Jackson called the Bank of the United States "a monster." He battled it vigorously, as this old cartoon shows, and finally subdued it. Jackson is the white-haired figure on the left, waving a sword. The monster's largest head, in the center wearing a top hat, is Nicholas Biddle of Philadelphia, the bank's president. (Library of Congress.)

McLane of Delaware became secretary of state; he also served briefly as secretary of the treasury, a post later filled by Roger Brooke Taney, a former member of the Kitchen Cabinet. Cary A. Harris of Tennessee served as secretary of war; Benjamin Franklin Butler of New York as attorney general; Amos Kendall of Kentucky as postmaster general; and Mahlon Dickerson of New Jersey as secretary of the navy. Some Cabinet positions changed hands during Jackson's second term. John Forsyth of Georgia became secretary of state midway through the term, and Levi Woodstock of New Hampshire took over the post of secretary of the treasury.

Victory Over "The Monster"

As soon as he was re-elected, Jackson took action against the Bank of the United States, not waiting until the charter came up for renewal in 1836. He appointed his friend Roger Taney as the secretary of the treasury and had Taney withdraw the government's deposits from the bank; they were then placed in various state banks.

Biddle fought back, getting Congress to pass an official censure, or statement of disapproval, against Jackson. He also tried to create a nationwide financial panic by demanding the repayment of loans that had been made by the bank. Biddle, Clay, and other supporters of the bank tried to stir up popular resentment against the President's strong-willed, single-minded control of the government. They circulated posters and handbills calling him "King Andrew I," and they referred to his administration as "the monarchy" and "the reign of King Andrew."

But the people's affection for Jackson did not waver. Tyrannical he may have been in some respects, high-handed he certainly was, but "King Andrew" retained the loyalty of the voters. And he stood firm against the bank. Biddle's measures to save the bank were unsuccessful, and its federal charter was withdrawn in 1836. Later, it failed to survive as a state bank, and Biddle retired to Philadelphia a bitter and defeated man.

Jackson's administration succeeded in destroying the Bank of the United States, but it did not succeed in developing a sound national banking policy. The government did not yet issue its own paper money, and Jackson continued to believe in gold and silver. One of his last acts as President was to issue a declaration that only hard money could be used to pay for purchases of land from the federal government. Partly as a result of this action, a financial panic swept across the nation in 1837, the year after Jackson left office. Hundreds of banks and businesses were forced to close and many people lost their jobs. Most Americans, however, did not blame the former President for the Panic of 1837.

Matters Foreign and Texan

Jackson's presidency is remembered chiefly for the problems of the Indians and the bank. But many other matters arose during his two terms in office, including a number of dealings with foreign powers.

Among them, Jackson was able to settle some old claims made by the United States against England and France for American property that had been seized during the Napoleonic Wars. He also negotiated an agreement with England that allowed free trade with the British islands in the Caribbean; these islands were an important source of sugar and rum and a significant market for goods manufactured in New England. Jackson also sent the first major American diplomatic mission to Southeast Asia and signed America's first treaty with the nation of Siam (present-day Thailand).

Jackson was not always a winner in foreign affairs, however. He was unable to settle an ongoing boundary dispute between Maine and Canada. He tried to buy Texas from Mexico, but failed. When the Mexicans would not even consider selling Texas, the Texans took matters into their own hands.

The Battle of the Alamo took place in March of 1836. A 3,000-man Mexican army captured the tiny fort and killed its 184 defenders, including frontiersman Davy Crockett, who had once marched in Jackson's militia. With the cry of "Remember the Alamo!" to urge them to victory, the Texans

The Texas Revolution

By the end of the 18th century, Spain's empire in the Americas was in decline. The area that is now Texas was then part of Spanish-owned Mexico, which had been colonized by Spain centuries earlier. But hostile Indians and a harsh environment had reduced the number of permanent Spanish settlements in Texas to three by 1800. A few years later, Napoleon I of France sold the Louisiana Territory to the United States. This meant that the United States now extended all the way to the border of Spanish-claimed territory in Texas. It also meant that many Americans began to look covetously toward Texas as settlement increased in the United States.

Much of Texas was almost empty in the early 1800s, so in 1821 Mexico, which that year had won its independence from Spain, decided to allow Americans to settle there. By 1835, in the middle of President Jackson's second term, about 20,000 U.S. settlers and about 4,000 slaves were living in Texas. Several times, the United States tried unsuccessfully to buy Texas from Mexico. These efforts, however, convinced the Mexican authorities that they had made a mistake in allowing Americans to enter the region. They then tried to stem the flow of settlers into Texas, but the colonists kept coming, drawn by the lure of wide-open land.

During Jackson's administration, the American colonists in Texas rebelled against the Mexican government. They claimed that their revolt was aimed at Mexican military dictator Antonio Lopez de Santa Anna and that they intended to remain part of Mexico after Santa Anna was overthrown. But most historians agree that the Texans really wanted independence.

The fighting broke out in October of 1835. After the Texans captured the Mexican stronghold of San Antonio, Texas, Santa Anna marched into Texas to crush the rebellion.

At first, Santa Anna had the upper hand. He massacred a Texan force near the city of Goliad, then he recaptured San Antonio. But the turning point of the rebellion—and its most famous incident—came when his 6,000-man army beseiged a mission-fortress called the Alamo near San Antonio.

General Sam Houston, who was a good friend of Jackson, had ordered the Texans to abandon the fort, fearing that they would not be able to defend it against Santa Anna. But the soldiers garrisoned there refused to leave their posts. On February 23, 1836, Santa Anna arrived in the San Antonio area and demanded the surrender of the Alamo. The handful of American defenders inside the fort refused to give it up. Under the command of Colonel William Barret Travis, the Texans and their allies, including Tennesseean Davy Crockett, prepared to defend the fort to the death.

Santa Anna waited for a week or so, then launched a massive attack against the Alamo on the morning of March 6. Mexican troops threw ladders against the fort's walls and scrambled up. Although the Texans fired down upon the climbers, killing hundreds of them, the Mexicans finally reached the inside of the fort. Bloody hand-to-hand fighting then raged for hours. Finally, all 183 of the Alamo's defenders were killed, but not before they had killed about 1,550 Mexicans.

The desperate seige and heroic Battle of the Alamo gave new life to the rebellion. Texans now cried "Remember the Alamo!" as they swore to throw off the hated Mexican oppressors. Meanwhile, Santa Anna was determined to restore Mexican control to the region. He pursued the Texan army to San Jacinto, near present-day Houston, and there the two forces met in battle about six weeks after the Battle of the Alamo. Under Houston's command, the Texans soundly defeated Santa Anna's army, which then retreated hastily and in disarray to Mexico.

Soon afterward, Texas declared itself an independent republic, with Houston as its president. Mexico refused to recognize the existence of the new republic, but it was unable to do anything about it. Texas was now no longer a part of Mexico—and most people believed that, before many years had passed, Texas would become part of the United States.

battled the Mexicans and declared their independence as the Lone Star Republic later that same year. Jackson was eager to recognize Texan independence and to welcome Texas into the Union, but he knew that he must proceed cautiously to prevent a war between Mexico and the United States. He waited until his last day in office, March 3, 1837, to grant full diplomatic recognition to the new republic.

Chapter 8
The Final Years

Jackson remarked in 1837, "After eight years as President I have only two regrets: that I have not shot Henry Clay or hanged John C. Calhoun." After his spirited battles with these two opponents, Old Hickory's final years in the President's House must have seemed rather tame. They were not, however, uneventful.

Soon after beginning his second term, Jackson received a doctor of law degree from Harvard College in Cambridge, Massachusetts. The degree was an honorary one, which meant that it was given in recognition of Jackson's public service rather than awarded after a formal course of study. Jackson, in fact, had never even been to Harvard. He accepted the honor with good grace, however, and was pleased and a little amused that the citadel of eastern polish and learning had granted a law degree to a President who had practiced his own brand of rough frontier law.

But John Quincy Adams, Jackson's old enemy, was neither pleased nor amused. He had graduated from Harvard, and he felt that Jackson did not deserve a Harvard degree. In a letter to the president of the college, Adams announced that he would not appear at the ceremony honoring Jackson: "As myself an affectionate child of our alma mater, I would not be present to witness her disgrace in conferring her highest

Jackson was the first President to be the target of an assassination attempt. The attempt failed, although the would-be assassin, a mentally ill house painter named Richard Lawrence, pulled two pistols on the startled President. Jackson appears in the left center of the drawing. (Library of Congress.)

literary honors upon a barbarian who could not write a sentence of grammar and hardly could spell his own name."

In 1835, Jackson made presidential history when he became the first American President to be the target of an assassin. Jackson was attending a funeral in Washington at the time. Richard Lawrence, a mentally disturbed house painter, ran up to the President and aimed a pistol at him, but the gun didn't fire. Lawrence then tried using a second pistol, but this one also failed to fire. The crowd seized the would-be assassin and Jackson was unharmed. Lawrence was found to be insane at the time of the attempted shooting and spent the rest of his life in jails and mental hospitals.

Jackson's last years in office saw the admission of two more states into the Union: Arkansas in June of 1836 and Michigan in January of 1837. There were now 26 states. In addition, the Wisconsin Territory was formally organized under the Jackson administration, and Jackson knew that before long it would contribute new states to the Union. The westward growth and expansion of the nation must have pleased Jackson, who had always been a fervent nationalist and westerner.

During his last year as President, Jackson suffered another personal loss. Emily Donelson, who was Rachel's niece and Andrew Jackson Donelson's wife, had been the official hostess in the President's House for most of Jackson's administration. All four of her children had been born in the President's House. In 1836, Emily developed tuberculosis and returned to Tennessee; soon after, she died. Her place as hostess in the President's House was taken by Sarah York Jackson, the wife of Jackson's adopted son.

After the original Hermitage was nearly gutted by fire in the early 1830s, Jackson had it rebuilt in preparation for his retirement. Visitors were impressed with its comfortable but refined interior. (Library of Congress.)

OUT OF THE SPOTLIGHT

During Jackson's final year in office, the President helped Martin Van Buren secure the Democratic nomination for the 1836 presidential election. Jackson was the first President who actively campaigned on behalf of his successor. Van Buren won, and many observers felt that he had been elected not because of his own abilities but because the people had great trust in Old Hickory's endorsement.

Van Buren's inauguration day in 1837 was a sort of farewell appearance for Jackson. Thomas Hart Benton, a U.S. senator from Missouri who Jackson had once threatened to horsewhip in Nashville but who had since become a friend and supporter of Jackson, was present at the inauguration. He said, "For once, the rising was eclipsed by the setting sun." Jackson made a speech to the crowd, reminding his audience of the sacred importance of the federal Union. He told them: "My own race is nearly run; advanced age and failing health warn me that before long I must pass beyond the reach of human events. . . . I bid you a last and affectionate farewell."

A few days later, Jackson began the long trip back to Tennessee and his home. He was almost 70 years old, thin and feeble, and in very poor health. But his spirits were lifted by the crowds that came to cheer him at every stop, just as they had cheered him on his way to Washington eight years before.

At The Hermitage

After the interior of The Hermitage had been severely damaged by a fire in the early 1830s, Jackson had the house rebuilt to suit his retirement plans. It was an elegant two-story building with tall white pillars in front and a sweeping, tree-lined carriage drive. The interior was furnished simply, but with high-quality materials and craftsmanship.

Jackson hoped to spend his remaining years in peace and quiet comfort at The Hermitage, but his homecoming was not entirely happy. He found that Andrew Jackson, Jr., the son he and Rachel had adopted in 1809, had managed the estate poorly and had run up many debts. Jackson was forced to spend considerable time and energy repairing the mansion and paying his debts. (The Hermitage passed into the possession of the state of Tennessee in 1856. It was fully restored in 1974 and is now a museum of Jackson's life and achievements.)

Jackson's health failed fast. He became almost deaf and lost the sight of one eye. He suffered constant discomfort from tuberculosis and from dropsy, a disease that caused his body to swell with fluids. He was sometimes unable to lie down and had to sleep propped up with pillows in his chair. As often as he could, however, he rode out on horseback by day to inspect his plantation. In the evening, he conducted family prayers. And he continued to take a lively interest in politics by reading newspapers, corresponding with friends in the government, and discussing the issues of the day with his local friends.

But Jackson was more than just an observer of politics during his final years. He continued to play a role as an advisor in the political scene. Van Buren consulted him often, asking his advice and opinions on a number of issues. Jackson was disappointed, however, that Van Buren refused to annex Texas as a state because he did not want to add another slave-holding state to the Union. Like many southerners, Jackson was a slave-holder and did not foresee the coming tragic conflict over the issue of slavery. Nonetheless, Jackson was sorry to see Van Buren lose his race for re-election in 1840.

When William Henry Harrison, a Whig, was elected President in 1840, Jackson said grimly that he hoped he would live long enough to see the Democrats return to power. Harrison died after less than a month in office, and his Vice-President, John Tyler, was more acceptable to Jackson because he had once been a Democrat.

Van Buren hoped to win the Democratic presidential nomination in 1844, but Jackson gave his endorsement to James Knox Polk of Tennessee, who then received the nomination. Jackson lived to see Polk win the presidential election, defeating Jackson's old enemy, Henry Clay.

Two events of the final months of Jackson's life brought him great pleasure. One was an act of Congress. In January of 1844, the House of Representatives voted 158 to 28 to refund the $1,000 fine Jackson had paid so many years ago for contempt of court in declaring martial law during the Battle of New Orleans. The money was returned to Jackson—with interest. What really made him happy, though, was that the refund was something like an apology from his countrymen and a recognition that he had been right, after all.

The other event that brightened Jackson's final days was the annexation of Texas into the Union. President Tyler began the process of making Texas part of the United States, and it was completed under Polk. Sam Houston, who had been a comrade in arms in the long-ago days of the Tennessee militia, was named the first governor of Texas. He and his son hurried to Nashville to share the news of his appointment with his old friend Jackson. Sadly, he arrived just hours after the former President's death on June 8, 1845. It is said that he threw himself weeping to his knees beside Jackson's coffin and told his son, "Try to remember that you have looked upon the face of Andrew Jackson."

Jackson died at age 78, surrounded by his friends, family, and servants. "I hope and trust to meet you all in Heaven, both white and black," he murmured to them shortly before his death. Hundreds of mourners wept at his funeral, grieving for the passing of a man who had been one of America's greatest heroes for 30 years. After an emotional service, Jackson was buried in the garden of The Hermitage, next to Rachel.

Chapter 9
Jacksonian Democracy

Jackson's eight years in office forever changed the nature of the presidency and of American democracy. Unlike many Presidents, he was more popular when he left office than when he entered it. This fact proved to many people that the movement called Jacksonian democracy was here to stay.

Jackson never fully understood the movement that came to bear his name. He was not given to political theorizing or to philosophy; he believed in Jacksonian democracy only because it supported him. But he did leave behind an enduring legacy of his belief in a truly broad American democracy, in which the voice of the ordinary farmer or factory worker is heard as clearly as that of the banker or merchant.

He also redefined the image of the popular President for generations to come. Earlier Presidents had been polished, well-educated easterners of good family. But Jackson gave the people pride in a new kind of President: the son of immigrants, born in humble and obscure circumstances, not university-educated or "book-learned," a frontiersman and a warrior. Jackson was an inspiring symbol of the self-made man and the virtues of the American frontier. More than any other President, he gave rise to the firm conviction among

Although he suffered from tuberculosis, dropsy, and other ailments, the aging Jackson retained his soldierly posture, his thick mane of hair, and his interest in political matters. The namesake of Jacksonian democracy died at The Hermitage in 1845. (Library of Congress.)

Americans that, indeed, everyone has the right to aspire to the highest office in the land.

Jackson also strengthened the role of the President. He refused to allow Congress or his Cabinet to make decisions for him. He vetoed 12 congressional bills, twice as many as the total vetoed by his six predecessors combined. He took more responsibility than any previous President for the direct management of the country. Following Jackson's presidency, no one thought of disputing the notion that the President, as the spokesman and representative of the people, should guide and direct the legislative and judicial branches of government.

Another legacy of Jackson's presidency was a flourishing two-party system. After the Federalist Party fell apart around 1817, the Democratic-Republicans had been the only real political party in the land. During the Jackson era, however, parties formed around major differences of opinion on important issues, such as states' rights. By the time Jackson left office, he and Van Buren and other Jacksonians had built a vigorous, well-organized Democratic Party, with many of the procedures and characteristics of today's political parties already in place. The Whigs were forced to become equally well-organized, and the two-party system never again fell out of use.

THE AGE OF JACKSON

Today, many historians refer to the period between the War of 1812 and the Civil War as the Age of Jackson. It was an era of growth and change in many ways. New technology was bringing new ways of traveling and working: Peter Cooper built the first American passenger locomotive; Thomas Davenport invented the electric motor and the electric print-

A Hero's Name

Heroes, warriors, and patriots throughout history have had cities named after them, but never was this practice more common than during the great period of American expansion in the 19th century. As settlers pushed westward, they gave their new towns names that honored or commemorated the people they most respected. Because Andrew Jackson was much loved as a fighter against the Indians and the British, the part of the United States that made up the frontier in the 1820s is dotted with cities bearing his name.

Perhaps the most famous of these is Jacksonville, Florida. It started as a small French settlement, then was held in turn by both the British and the Spanish. When the United States acquired Florida in 1821, the settlement was renamed in honor of Jackson, the new territory's first governor.

Another Jacksonville is located in Illinois; it was founded and named in 1825. To the south is Jackson, Mississippi, the capital of the state. It was laid out in 1822 and named for Jackson because he had negotiated with the Choctaw Indians for the land on which it stood. The northernmost Jackson is in Michigan. It started out in 1829 as a village called Jacksonborough, after the Indian fighter and hero of New Orleans. The name was soon changed to Jacksonopolis, but this name proved to be only temporary as well. In 1833, the town was renamed Jackson, and the name became permanent.

> Finally, Jackson's adopted state of Tennessee, not to be left out of the name game, has a city named Jackson. One of Rachel Jackson's nephews helped found the city, which was originally called Alexandria. In 1823, its name was changed to Jackson. It is certain that Jackson, who always encouraged growth in the West, was proud of the honor shown him by the citizens of this and the other new western towns that carried his name.

ing press; and in 1834 Cyrus H. McCormick patented the reaping machine, which was to cause a revolution in farming methods and help reduce the economic usefulness of slavery.

The temper of the times is reflected in the new writers who dominated the literary scene. No longer did Americans confine themselves to English or French classics. Authors like Nathaniel Hawthorne and Herman Melville wrote about Amerian life and people. One of the most popular authors of the period was James Fenimore Cooper, whose novels were truly Jacksonian in tone. In such books as *The Last of the Mohicans* and *The Pioneers*, Cooper fed the growing appetite for tales of the frontier and the rugged individuals who were leading America's march across the continent.

The Age of Jackson also saw a great increase in the number of people who participated in American life. Not only did the population of the United States grow, but new states were added to the Union, and their settlers and backwoodsmen became citizens. And, as property requirements were removed, more people from the laboring and farming classes became eligible to vote. In addition, many Americans had a greater interest in voting. Jackson had aroused the people to an awareness of their political power. He had given them a party structure that encouraged and promoted grass-roots participation in politics. And he had given them a personal hero to support with passion.

In Jackson's own words, spoken in his farewell speech at Van Buren's inauguration but addressed to all the people of the nation: "In your hands is rightfully placed the sovereignty of the country, and to you everyone placed in authority is ultimately responsible. It is always in your power to see that the wishes of the people are carried into faithful execution; . . . and while the people remain, as I trust they ever will, uncorrupted and uncorruptible, and continue watchful and jealous of their rights, the Government is safe, and the cause of freedom will continue to triumph over all its enemies."

Bibliography

Brown, Richard Holbrook. *The Hero and the People: The Meaning of Jacksonian Democracy.* New York: Macmillan, 1964. This is a short, easy-to-read, illustrated book that tells how Jackson appealed to the common people of his time and gave rise to a broader-based democracy in America.

Burke, Davis. *Old Hickory: The Life of Andrew Jackson.* New York: Dial Press, 1977. This lengthy but complete and colorfully illustrated biography also includes a bibliography of many additional books and articles. It is a good general-purpose volume for anyone who wants to read a single authoritative book about Jackson.

Horn, Stanley Fitzgerald. *The Hermitage: A History and Guide.* Nashville: Ladies' Hermitage Association, 1960. This 226-page illustrated guide to Jackson's home is fascinating reading, but it may be more detailed than some readers want. A 74-page version, prepared by the Ladies' Hermitage Association and published in 1964, is available in many libraries. It includes photos, drawings, and floor plans, as well as anecdotes about the house and its owner.

Lindsey, David. *Andrew Jackson and John C. Calhoun.* New York: Barron's Educational Series, 1973. Part of a series called "Shapers of History," this book chronicles the often stormy relationship between Jackson and his temperamental and ambitious Vice-President. It gives a vivid, detailed glimpse of the inner workings of our government and of two memorable politicians.

Marquis, James. *Andrew Jackson, the Border Captain*. New York: Grosset and Dunlap, 1933. This long but lively biography tells of Jackson's childhood, his education, his rip-roaring years as a frontier lawyer, and his military campaigns. It carries the story of his life up to 1821.

Marquis, James. *Andrew Jackson: Portrait of a President*. New York: Grosset and Dunlap, 1938. The second volume of Marquis' biography tells the story of Jackson the statesman and talks about Jacksonian democracy.

Mason, Van Wyck. *The Battles for New Orleans*. Boston: Houghton, Mifflin, 1962. The author is considered one of America's foremost writers of history, and this book shows us why. Only 183 pages long (with illustrations), it is an absorbing account of our nation's early history as it affected the colorful port city on the Mississippi River. The account of Jackson's defense of the city in 1815 is dramatic and exciting.

Remini, Robert V., editor. *The Age of Jackson, 1767–1845*. Columbia, South Carolina: University of South Carolina Press, 1972. Edited by a scholar of Jackson's life and times, this collection of essays discusses various aspects of the Jackson era: arts and literature, technology, political philosophy, and the effect of Jacksonian democracy.

Remini, Robert V. *Andrew Jackson*. Boston: Twayne, 1966. Part of a series called "Rulers and Statesmen of the World," this is a fairly compact (212 pages) and readable general account of Jackson's life.

Rozwenc, Edwin D., editor. *The Meaning of Jacksonian Democracy: Problems in American Civilization*. Boston: D. C. Heath, 1963. This is a very short volume of essays about the impact of Jackson's new brand of democracy on American history and politics. The introduction contains a good description of what is generally meant by Jacksonian democracy.

Viola, Herbert. *Andrew Jackson*. New York: Chelsea House, 1986. This short, easy-to-read biography was written especially for younger readers and is heavily illustrated.

Index

Adams, John, 61
Adams, John Quincy, 55, 56,
    61-63, 65, 69, 71, 99
Age of Jackson, 109-112
Alabama, 48
Alabama River, 45
Alamo, 94, 96-97
Amelia Island, 52
American Revolution, 14-16, 20,
    39, 71
Anti-Masonic Party, 66, 90
Appalachian Mountains, 18
Arkansas, 86, 101
Army, U.S., 2, 48, 84
Assassination attempt, 101
Avery, Waightstill, 29

Baltimore, Maryland, 89
Bank of the United States, 87-89,
    90, 93
Barataria, 3
Battle of Hanging Rock, 15
Bean, Russell, 27
Benton, Jesse, 31
Benton, Thomas Hart, 31-32, 103
Berrien, John M., 77
Berry, William T., 77
Biddle, Nicholas, 87, 93
Black militiamen, 3
Blair, Francis, 77
Blockade, 41
Blount, Willie, 25, 45
Boarding school, 14
Burr, Aaron, 36-39, 42
Butler, Benjamin Franklin, 92

Cabinet, 77, 88
Calhoun, John C., 99
    as a presidential candidate, 61, 62
    quarrel with Jackson and Van
        Buren, 77-82
    resignation of, 84
    as secretary of war, 54
    as a U.S. senator, 83
    as Vice-President, 65, 77
Callava, Jose, 58
Camden, South Carolina, 15
Campaign of 1824, 61-62
Campaign of 1828, 66-69
Campaign of 1832, 89-90
Canada, 94
Capitol, U.S., 71
Caribbean Sea, 2, 94
Carrickfergus, 11
Carroll, William, 31
Charleston, South Carolina, 15-16
Charlotte, North Carolina, 16
Cholera, 16
Citizenship, U.S., 41
Civil servants, 76
Clay, Henry, 97
    and the Bank of the United
        States, 87
    and the Force Bill, 82-84
    as a presidential candidate, 61,
        62, 90, 105
    as Speaker of the House, 62-63
    and states' rights, 82
Clover Bottom, 33
Commercial treaties, 94
Congress, U.S., 10, 26, 36, 42, 88
Constitution, U.S., 73, 78

115

PRESIDENTS OF THE UNITED STATES

GEORGE WASHINGTON	L. Falkof	0-944483-19-4
JOHN ADAMS	R. Stefoff	0-944483-10-0
THOMAS JEFFERSON	R. Stefoff	0-944483-07-0
JAMES MADISON	B. Polikoff	0-944483-22-4
JAMES MONROE	R. Stefoff	0-944483-11-9
JOHN QUINCY ADAMS	M. Greenblatt	0-944483-21-6
ANDREW JACKSON	R. Stefoff	0-944483-08-9
MARTIN VAN BUREN	R. Ellis	0-944483-12-7
WILLIAM HENRY HARRISON	R. Stefoff	0-944483-54-2
JOHN TYLER	L. Falkof	0-944483-60-7
JAMES K. POLK	M. Greenblatt	0-944483-04-6
ZACHARY TAYLOR	D. Collins	0-944483-17-8
MILLARD FILLMORE	K. Law	0-944483-61-5
FRANKLIN PIERCE	F. Brown	0-944483-25-9
JAMES BUCHANAN	D. Collins	0-944483-62-3
ABRAHAM LINCOLN	R. Stefoff	0-944483-14-3
ANDREW JOHNSON	R. Stevens	0-944483-16-X
ULYSSES S. GRANT	L. Falkof	0-944483-02-X
RUTHERFORD B. HAYES	N. Robbins	0-944483-23-2
JAMES A. GARFIELD	F. Brown	0-944483-63-1
CHESTER A. ARTHUR	R. Stevens	0-944483-05-4
GROVER CLEVELAND	D. Collins	0-944483-01-1
BENJAMIN HARRISON	R. Stevens	0-944483-15-1
WILLIAM McKINLEY	D. Collins	0-944483-55-0
THEODORE ROOSEVELT	R. Stefoff	0-944483-09-7
WILLIAM H. TAFT	L. Falkof	0-944483-56-9
WOODROW WILSON	D. Collins	0-944483-18-6
WARREN G. HARDING	A. Canadeo	0-944483-64-X
CALVIN COOLIDGE	R. Stevens	0-944483-57-7

HERBERT C. HOOVER	B. Polikoff	0-944483-58-5
FRANKLIN D. ROOSEVELT	M. Greenblatt	0-944483-06-2
HARRY S. TRUMAN	D. Collins	0-944483-00-3
DWIGHT D. EISENHOWER	R. Ellis	0-944483-13-5
JOHN F. KENNEDY	L. Falkof	0-944483-03-8
LYNDON B. JOHNSON	L. Falkof	0-944483-20-8
RICHARD M. NIXON	R. Stefoff	0-944483-59-3
GERALD R. FORD	D. Collins	0-944483-65-8
JAMES E. CARTER	D. Richman	0-944483-24-0
RONALD W. REAGAN	N. Robbins	0-944483-66-6
GEORGE H.W. BUSH	R. Stefoff	0-944483-67-4

GARRETT EDUCATIONAL CORPORATION
130 EAST 13TH STREET
ADA, OK 74820